The DIY GUIDE *to* FREE PUBLICITY

100+ Things You Can Do to
Get Media Coverage
for Your Business **NOW**

Christina Daves

Copyright © 2020 by Christina Daves

No part of this publication may be reproduced, distributed, or transmitted in any form or by any means, including photocopying, recording, or other electronic or mechanical methods, or by any information storage and retrieval system without the prior written permission of the publisher, except in the case of very brief quotations embodied in critical reviews and certain other noncommercial uses permitted by copyright law.

Monarch Crown Publishing
www.monarchcrownpublishing.com

All Rights Reserved.
ISBN ebook: 978-1-7340538-0-7
ISBN Print book: 978-1-7340538-2-1

You never know where life will take you.
Hold on and enjoy the journey.

Thank you, Steve, Justin and Megan for sharing all of this with me. Everything in life is so much greater because of each of you.

Foreword

If you're reading this book, you're probably excited about providing value to others and sharing your message with the world. You want to share your gifts, but might not have a clear vision of how to do so. What's so great about *The DIY Guide to FREE Publicity* is that Christina lays out a myriad of tips, tricks, and strategies to help people from all industries become a master of their message and increase their credibility exponentially. And I can vouch that these techniques work because I've not only seen their results firsthand, but I also use them myself.

In fact, I'd like to tell you about the first time I ever met Christina, which was a direct result of her dedication to generating publicity and credibility. I was traveling to D.C. and Baltimore on business and wanted to record a few episodes of my podcast for Entrepreneur Magazine, The Playbook, while I was in the area, I had reached out to one of my good friends to see if he had any recommendations for potential guests and there was one person in particular that he said I had to meet...Christina Daves. What struck me upon meeting her (apart from her energy) was when I discovered just how aligned we were when it came to matters of marketing, branding, and PR.

My experience working with world-class athletes as the former CEO of the renowned Leigh Steinberg Sports & Entertainment agency and CEO of Sports 1 Marketing had helped me to understand the world of branding and public relations as they related to sports, but it was only when I began building my own personal brand that I realized how important it is to take control of your own message. Remember, nobody is as passionate about you or your business as you are. That's why you need to take the impetus to generate publicity for yourself!

We all have a frequency, a vibration that is an emotional appeal meant to connect us with the rest of the world, and nobody understands your frequency better than you do. To truly resonate with others, our messages need to be authentic, truthful, and consistent. When I met Christina for the podcast, we talked about things like increasing your visibility, combining traditional and digital mediums to get the most out of PR opportunities, and the necessity of making adjustments, all topics that are mentioned in this book.

What these ideas boil down to is that PR strategy is based on elevating awareness. As you'll read, Visibility = Customers = Profit, which is why the lessons that Christina shares are so crucial; these strategies will help elevate others awareness of you and the value that you have to provide. Many of the techniques mentioned in *The DIY Guide to FREE Publicity* are about what I call "planting the right seeds." In order to create or build anything, we need to start with imagination. Envision the outcomes you want, your "what," and then do the work to get there. You've got to nurture the seeds you plant in order to eventually harvest them. What this book does is help you to select the right seeds for your goals, teaches you how to nurture and fertilize them, and when to harvest. You'll learn how to do everything, from branding yourself with the right website, to building relationships with journalists, pitching, leveraging video content, and much more.

Christina's tips in this book are a great guide to help you build your brand and its visibility, sharing your value (and frequency) with the world, while also making a lasting impact on your business. No matter the industry you operate in or the goals you might have, you will be able to take these strategies and apply them to be successful. When you are able to think, say, do, and believe the right things when it comes to your own PR campaigns, then it will yield the results you desire. **– David Meltzer, CEO and Co-Founder, Sports1 Marketing**

Why fit in when you were born to stand out?
~ Dr. Seuss

Table of Contents

INTRODUCTION PINCH ME! 1
THE SECRET TO GETTING AHEAD IS GETTING STARTED ~ MARK TWAIN 5
    TIP #1 – WHAT'S YOUR WHY? 6
    TIP #2 – YOUR BRANDING IS YOUR EVERYTHING 6
    TIP #3 – ARE YOU LIVING UP TO YOUR NAME? 7
    TIP #4 – IT'S TIME TO STOCKPILE 9
    TIP #5 – IF YOU BUILD IT, THEY WILL COME 9
    TIP #6 – DOMAIN DEAL...10
    TIP #7 – YOUR CALLING CARD...11
    TIP #8 – A PICTURE IS WORTH A THOUSAND WORDS .12
    TIP #9 – TRUSTWORTHINESS 14
    TIP #10 – THERE IS ONLY ONE BOSS 14
    TIP #11 – WHAT FLOOR? 15
    TIP #12 – KNOWLEDGE IS POWER......................................16
    TIP #13 – BE AUTHENTIC 17
    TIP #14 – IT'S A WRAP 18
MAKE A NAME FOR YOURSELF..19
    TIP #15 – SHOUT IT FROM THE ROOFTOPS 20
    TIP #16 – ALWAYS PROVIDE VALUE FIRST 22
    TIP #17 – THE GIVING TREE 23
    TIP #18 – AND THE WINNER IS…..25
    TIP #19 – THE AWARD GOES TO…......................................27
    TIP #20 – IT'S PARTYTIME 28
    TIP #21 – GET A FREE RIDE 29
    TIP #22 – ALERT! 29
    TIP #23 – WHO'S TALKING ABOUT YOU? 31

TIP #24 – YOUR FOOTPRINT IN THE SAND 32

GET PR FAMOUS FORMULA 35

TIP #25 – PAID VS. EARNED 36
TIP #26 – FOR IMMEDIATE RELEASE 37
TIP #27 – ACTION! 38
TIP #28 – PITCH PERFECT 39
TIP #29 – WHO CARES? 39
TIP #30 – MAKE YOUR MARK 40
TIP #31 – PAPARAZZI 41
TIP #32 – COME BEARING GIFTS 41
TIP #33 – COLLABORATE 43
TIP #34 – PRACTICE MAKES PERFECT 44

Make it Work for You 45

TIP #35 – HOW FAST CAN THIS GO? 46
TIP #36 – TELL THE WORLD YOU'RE HERE! 47
TIP #37 – GO BEYOND THE BOX 48
TIP #38 – BE NEW-SWORTHY 48
TIP #39 – NICHE THE PITCH 50
TIP #40 – MEDIA BEGETS MEDIA 51
TIP #41 – SEASONALITY 52
TIP #42 – DAVID VS. GOLIATH 53
TIP #43 – BE NON-TRADITIONAL 53
TIP #44 – DO YOUR HOMEWORK 55
TIP #45 – CELEBRITY SELLS 56
TIP #46 – WHAT'S THE STORY? 57
TIP #47 – THE ART OF THE HOOK 58
TIP #48 – COVER STORY 58
TIP #49 – COMING UP NEXT… 59
TIP #50 – WHERE ARE YOU? 60

We Want YOU! 61

TIP #51 – HELP A REPORTER OUT 62
TIP #52 – PITCHRATE 64
TIP #53 – SOURCE BOTTLE 65
TIP #54 – QWOTED 65

TABLE OF CONTENTS · ix

TIP #55 – JOURNOREQUESTS 66
TIP #56 – DON'T BE LATE 66
TIP #57 – DON'T GO "FISHING" 67
TIP #58 – K.I.S.S 67
TIP #59 – BE KIND 68
TIP #60 – NO PHOTOS PLEASE...69
TIP #61 – TWEET, TWEET 69

THE ROAD TO STARDOM 71

TIP #62 – ARE YOU THE ONE? 72
TIP #63 – MAKE IT EPIC! 73
TIP #64 – WHAT'S NEWSWORTHY WHEN? 74
TIP #65 – TIMELY TRENDS 75
TIP #66 – WHAT'S OLD IS NEW AGAIN..................................76
TIP #67 – BE A STAR 76
TIP #68 – DON'T PITCH A PITCH..77
TIP #69 – BEST OF THE BEST 77
TIP #70 – DON'T FORGET THE LITTLE GUY 78
TIP #71 – FLY AWAY WITH ME 79
TIP #72 – PLAN AHEAD 81
TIP #73 – HO HO HOLIDAYS 81
TIP #74 – MARK YOUR CALENDAR 82
TIP #75 – BE TIMELY 82
TIP #76 – TO WHOM DO YOU SEND IT? 83
TIP #77 – IT'S THAT EASY 84
TIP #78 – ANYONE, ANYWHERE...85
TIP #79 – GO WITH WHAT YOU KNOW 85
TIP #80 – SEND A SPECIAL PACKAGE 86
TIP #81 – A SIDE JOB 86
TIP #82 – STOP THE PRESSES! 87

YOUR NAME IN LIGHTS..89

TIP #83 – START AT HOME 90
TIP #84 – WHO, WHAT, WHEN, WHERE? 92
TIP #85 – THINK BIG, START SMALL......................................92
TIP #86 – GO FOR IT 93

TIP #87 – YOUR "SIZZLE" 96
TIP #88 – MAKE IT EASY FOR THEM 96
TIP #89 – BE OUR GUEST 97
TIP #90 – CHECK THE CLASSIFIEDS 97
TIP #91 – HARO-ING FOR TV 98
TIP #92 – SOCIAL "NETWORKING" 98
TIP #93 – WHERE DO I FIND YOU? 99
TIP #94 – WHERE DO YOU FIT IN THE PUZZLE? 101
TIP #95 – NO STALKING PLEASE 102
TIP #96 – PAY TO "PLAY" 103
TIP #97 – IT'S ALL ABOUT YOU 103
TIP #98 – POLISH YOUR PITCH WITH THE PRO 106
TIP #99 – LEARNING TO TALK 108
TIP #100 – YA'LL COME BACK NOW 109
TIP #101 – WORST-CASE SCENARIO 110
TIP #102 – LOOKING GOOD 111
TIP #103 – WHAT TO WEAR WHERE 112
TIP #104 – YOU GOT THE AXE 113
TIP #105 – COPY THAT 114
TIP #106 – RIDE THE WAVE 115
TIP #107 – WHAT'S YOUR REALITY? 116
TIP #108 – PRODUCT PLACEMENT 118

RADIO-ACTIVE 121

TIP #109 – PODCASTER'S PARADISE 121
TIP #110 – WHAT'S YOUR STORY? 123
TIP #111 – FOLLOW THE RULES 124
TIP #112 – IT'S FREE HERE TOO 124
TIP #113 – HOW DO I FIND YOU? 124
TIP #114 – FOR STARTERS 125
TIP #115 – TALK THE TALK 126
TIP #116 – GIVE A GIFT 127

CONTENT IS KING 129

TIP #117 – LET'S GET THIS PARTY STARTED 130
TIP #118 – ONCE IS ENOUGH 131

- TIP #119 – GIVE THEM WHAT THEY WANT 131
- TIP #120 – BE A DIAMOND IN THE ROUGH 132
- TIP #121 – BE A GUEST 132
- TIP #122 – SOCIAL BUTTERFLY 133
- TIP #123 – PAY IT FORWARD 133
- TIP #124 – THE ROAD LESS TRAVELED 134
- TIP #125 – STATS 101 135

YOU'RE INVITED TO A COCKTAIL PARTY 137
- TIP #126 – WHAT IS IT ANYWAY? 138
- TIP #127 – ZUCKERBERG'S BABY 139
- TIP #128 – GOING LIVE 140
- TIP #129 – BLUE BIRD CAFÉ 141
- TIP #130 – PIN-IT 142
- TIP #131 – FREEZE-FRAME 143
- TIP #132 – TELL ME A STORY 145
- TIP #133 – ARE YOU LINKED IN? 145
- TIP #134 – GOING TUBING 147
- TIP #135 – AUTOMATION NATION 149
- TIP #136 – 80/20 RULE 150

EXTRA! EXTRA! 151
- TIP #137 – I THINK I CAN! I THINK I CAN! 151
- TIP #138 – WHAT'S THE WORST THAT CAN HAPPEN? 153
- TIP #139 – WHEN A "NO" ISN'T NO 154
- TIP #140 – DRIP, DRIP, DRIP 155
- TIP #141 – IT'S ALL ABOUT THEM 156
- TIP #142 – WHAT'S YOUR PLAN? 157
- TIP #143 – NICE TO MEET YOU 157
- TIP #144 – ONCE IS NOT ENOUGH 158
- TIP #145 – CONNECT, CONNECT, CONNECT 159
- TIP #146 – THANK YOU VERY MUCH 159
- TIP #147 – BEHIND THE CURTAIN 160

THANKS FOR YOUR TIME… 161
ABOUT THE AUTHOR 163

Free Gift for Readers of This Book

For all the special resources in this book, go to
www.PRforAnyone.com/BookResources

Introduction
Pinch Me!

When I released the first version of this book, *PR for Anyone 100+ Affordable Ways to Easily Create Buzz for Your Business*, I only had my own stories to share. I knew what worked for me, but would it work for others? I've learned so much since then and can't wait to share it with you.

Here's how my story started...

I invented a product, fashion accessories for medical boots, and I hired a "retail expert" to help me get them manufactured and to market. This guy was a smooth talker but had no idea what he was actually talking about. He took advantage of me to the tune of $27,000! I got zero results. The positive spin on this was that I was now completely broke so I couldn't hire a PR firm or buy any advertising even if I wanted to (this really was a positive). So, I had to figure out how to do my own publicity and guess what? I was pretty darn good at it.

In my first year in business, I appeared in over 50 media outlets, including nationally syndicated shows such as *Steve Harvey and Dr. Oz* as well as local *FOX*, *NBC*, and *CBS* affiliates, *The Washington Post*, *Parenting Magazine*, and many others -- all in the first year of business! To date I've appeared in over 1,000 media outlets and even have a regular television segment on ABC in Washington, D.C. Sometimes I have to pinch myself to believe this is really my life now.

I figured out a system that I call my Get PR Famous Formula. It works, and it works consistently for just about anyone in any industry. In one year, the people I worked with had almost a billion views and over eight figures in sales from free publicity. Some of these people spent tens of thousands of dollars on PR firms in the past with few or no results. It's in the fine print of the PR firm's contract. They don't guarantee media placement. That's why learning how to create your own media strategy and then implementing it in-house is so important.

Landing publicity should be a regular part of your marketing plan.

I know of no better way to get massive exposure for your business at no cost. It's simple: Visibility = Customers = Profits. The key, however, is consistency. You want to be pitching the same journalists different story ideas every single month so you become front of mind with them about your industry. Imagine what it will be like when they call you for a story.

Publicity gives you instant credibility. It positions you as an authority in your industry. There is the presumption that if you are covered by the media, you must be good at what you do. This credibility opens doors, gets you in front of potential clients, and helps you close the deal because you are perceived as a leading expert in your space.

DIY publicity is simple - if you follow the system.

It works for seasoned veterans and people brand new to an industry. Once you understand how the system works, pitching the media will take less than ten minutes per day. Would ten minutes be worth a million new people learning about you and your business? I know of no other way to get in front of that many potential new customers, at no charge, than publicity. It also elevates your authority, your credibility, and ultimately your income.

It's been almost seven years since I launched PR for Anyone® and over five years since I published my first book. A lot has changed since then. That's why I gave the old book an overhaul. I added new tips, updated old tips, and am sharing real-world case studies so you can see how the people I've worked with landed in the media. Hopefully this sparks your creativity on how to pitch good stories.

I walk this walk every single day in my own business and am living proof that anyone can learn the basics of do-it-yourself publicity, develop a strategy, build relationships, and get great results!

The Secret To Getting Ahead is Getting Started ~ Mark Twain

You know you have a great business, but it's your competitor who is always grabbing the spotlight, landing the media exposure, the leads, and the customers. You're probably asking yourself, "How are they doing this?"

I hear it all the time: *I don't even know the first thing when it comes to PR.* Guess what? I didn't either. Now that I do, I'm going to share it all with you, and even include tips from industry experts to help you land publicity.

This I know for certain: media today is 24/7/365. They need story ideas. In fact, I'd say the media needs us as much as we need them, maybe more. They are filling airtime, print, and websites with content. If you can consistently give them good story ideas, they will welcome you into their tribe.

At first, getting publicity seems elusive, even scary. I assure you this initial "fear-of-the-unknown" will pass quickly, especially once you start seeing results.

You may not think these first tips relate to public relations, but they are absolutely crucial in building your overall image, brand, and ultimately, your PR.

If you've followed me for some time, you know that I always wear pink. I wear pink when I speak. I wear pink when I'm on television. I wear pink whenever I shoot videos. Anywhere someone might go to learn about me such as my websites or social media platforms is consistent with my branding so there is never a question whether or not it is me.

Your brand and anything that represents you or your company is vital to your PR efforts. You must be professional, expert-worthy, and someone the media would want to share with their audience. Remember, the media will check you out before they use you so let's make sure you check out.

Relax and let's get started...

TIP #1 – WHAT'S YOUR WHY?

When your why is big enough you will find your how.
~ Les Brown

Since I started coaching clients on gaining visibility, the very first question I ask them is, "Why are you doing what you're doing?" Your story is what the media wants to learn about and without knowing *why* you do what you do, you can't fully tell your story. This is the most critical question to your business and ultimately to your PR efforts.

TIP #2 – YOUR BRANDING IS YOUR EVERYTHING

A brand for a company is like a reputation for a person.
~ Jeff Bezos

Branding your business is important because it communicates to the world what your business represents and who you are. Basically, your brand is your reputation.

You want your branding to be consistent across everything you do. It starts with your logo and goes from your website, to your blog, to your social media, to your business cards. Everything you submit to the media about your business should be consistent. Use the same logo, the same fonts, and the same marketing messages. Design templates that are all similar, using the same logo placement and color schemes. If you have a tagline, use it in everything.

As I mentioned, pink is my signature color. People know that I am the "PR Coach in Pink" so there is brand association with pink and my business. Remember, every aspect of your business should reinforce the other parts.

MY FAVORITE TIP – Become known for something in your industry. Establish a niche and differentiate yourself so you can stand out among others in your field.

TIP #3 – ARE YOU LIVING UP TO YOUR NAME?

> *What's in a name? That which we call a rose*
> *by any other name would smell as sweet.*
> *~ William Shakespeare*

You absolutely must own your business domain name. If someone else already has it, reconsider the name of your business. There are variations you can use. However, I recommend against using a hyphenated domain name or a name with an extension such as, LLC. It's too complicated and makes it difficult to differentiate yourself.

If you do decide to go the hyphen or extension route, be certain that the other website using your actual business domain name is one you would be okay with your customers or the media visiting. Odds are, at some point, they will land on that page inadvertently. If it's a direct competitor or someone who sells something that may be offensive, you should reconsider.

There are, however, unique ways to use your business name in a domain that can be effective. When I owned a brick and mortar store, *Details for the Home*, we tried to secure the domain, www.detailsforthehome.com. Someone had already purchased it, but they weren't using it and there were no auctions at that time to try to secure the domain. Since we were a retail store, we opted to use www.ShopatDetails.com, which worked for what we were doing.

Next, ask yourself if your domain name is easy to remember? If not, find one that is. Remember to make sure it's pertinent to your business as we did with Details using "shop at." Even if you're already doing business with an overly complicated name, just forward the new, easy-to-remember domain name to your existing website. This way, nothing changes except the odds that you'll gain more visitors.

When I started my current company, I loved the name my friends helped me come up with, CastMedic Designs. It was a perfect description of the product. It left room to expand the line. Best of all, it's my initials, "CMD." Perfect, right? Well, not so much.

Over time, and with increased media appearances, I realized it was in fact, a terrible name! It's hard to remember, difficult to say, and even harder to spell. I cringed when I watched the recording of my appearance on the *Steve Harvey Show,* as he awkwardly pronounced my business name. CastMedic Designs doesn't exactly roll off the tongue.

I now own the domain, www.HealinStyle.com. It's perfect for TV, radio, or just in conversation. It's memorable and I have it set up to forward to www.CastMedicDesigns.com. This way, I didn't lose any online credibility already established with the original domain.

Also, try to get your name as a domain. I own www.Christina Daves.com, which is now the hub of my businesses. People want to work with people, not necessarily a company.

MY FAVORITE TIP – Don't forget variations and misspellings of your domain name. For example, I also own the domain, www.HeelinStyle.com, which is also forwarded to the main CastMedic Designs website. Cover all of your bases with possible spelling issues. You want people to find you.

TIP #4 – IT'S TIME TO STOCKPILE

Don't worry about failure; you only have to be right once
~ Drew Houston

Custom domain names are one of the easiest ways to direct people to different parts of your business or as a list building or lead generation tool. When you send someone to your domain name and then a backslash and then another name, it gets confusing. I have custom domains like ChatwithChristina.com if you'd like to set up a call with me or FreeGiftFromChristina.com for a media freebie I giveaway. I own 3StepstoPRSuccess.com, PublicityToolkit.com and hundreds of others. Think about easy URL's related to your business that you can secure. You don't need to use them right away, but keep them stockpiled in your marketing arsenal.

TIP #5 – IF YOU BUILD IT, THEY WILL COME

Be a yardstick of quality. Some people aren't used to
an environment where excellence is expected.
~ Steve Jobs

It's time to start building your brand. Maybe you already have a logo, but your message is inconsistent throughout other parts of your business. Maybe you haven't started yet or you've got some things going or you need to start over. It's important to get everything working together.

Whatever the case may be, there are several inexpensive online resources to help you with logo design, graphics, and templates.

One of my favorite resources is www.Fiverr.com. where you can get just about anything done for right around $5.00. A great printing resource is Got Print at www.GotPrint.com. You can purchase 1,000 business cards for around $40.00, including shipping. I also love the specials you can find at Vistaprint, www.VistaPrint.com.

MY FAVORITE TIP – Sign up for the print companies' mailing lists as they frequently email percentage off offers.

TIP #6 – DOMAIN DEAL

The way to wealth depends on just two words,
industry and frugality.
~ Benjamin Franklin

There are many companies that offer domain services. My recommendation is to go with one where you can house all of your domains in one location. My favorite is Go Daddy at www.GoDaddy.com. As I mentioned, I own hundreds of domains that I don't always have active so having them housed in one location is ideal.

Depending on how many domains you have, or plan to have, you can start out with discounts on individual domain names. Go to Google and enter "Go Daddy coupon." You can usually find a coupon for a discounted annual fee for a domain name. If you plan to have many domains, look into their bulk purchasing program. You pay an annual fee to be able to purchase and renew domains at a discounted rate. This is what I currently do and it pays for itself with the number of domains I own.

TIP #7 – YOUR CALLING CARD

Quality is not an act, it is a habit.
~ Aristotle

Have you ever gone to a website and thought, *"Ugh,"* or tried to find a business online that didn't have a website?

In today's age of immediate access to everything, not having a business website negatively affects your credibility. People want to see with whom they're dealing, and a website is the best way to do that.

As a consumer, if you're deciding between two places to buy something, or which company to hire, odds are, you are going to choose the one that presents itself better, the one that looks more professional.

Websites are incredibly affordable now so there is no excuse not to have one. You can find the top-rated website builders at www.Top10BestWebsiteBuilders.com.

There are also sites such as www.Upwork.com and www.99Designs.com where graphic design freelancers bid on winning your business. You join for free, submit a proposal for a job, and freelancers send their qualifications along with their bid. Then you simply hire the one you think is the best freelancer for your job. You escrow money for the project through the online company and don't pay until you are satisfied.

Don't discount Craig's List, www.CraigsList.com. There are a great many talented people posting freelance services there as well.

The single most important piece of advice in this book, and the best thing you can do for your PR, is to make sure the face of your business screams "professional" and "expert"! Let the world know that you are the best.

When you submit a story idea or an expert request to a journalist, the first thing they will likely do is visit your website and social media pages. They need to make sure you are someone they should write about or source. If you don't have a website or it's not projecting professionalism and expertise in your industry, they are not going to want to use you for their story.

It's also important to make sure your social media cover pages are created professionally. These graphics can be done easily and economically at www.Fiverr.com.

Remember, every part of your online presence is representing you - so make yourself look good!

TIP #8 – A PICTURE IS WORTH A THOUSAND WORDS

Just like your online presence, your photographs represent you and your business. I encourage you to invest in high-resolution, high-quality photographs for publicity. An immediate media opportunity could present itself and require high-resolution photos. You want to represent your product and your company with good, high-quality images. This type of photography is not expensive and something you will use over and over again.

If you are a product-based business, have quality shots taken on a white background that can be used by the media. Using a white background is standard in the industry, making it easy for you to send an acceptable sample photo of your product to a journalist. They will usually request high-resolution photos they can use rather than having you send the product for photographing.

This happened to me with *Vail Beaver Creek Magazine*. I had pitched a story and didn't hear back for a year. Then, they were running a story about Olympic Gold Medalist, Picabo Street, who had just broken her foot. The journalist had kept my pitch about the medical boot accessories, and they included me in the story. It was very last minute and I needed to provide high-resolution images for the magazine.

I didn't know it at the time, but the best money I invested early on was for creating high-quality product shots for my website. I have used these photographs hundreds of times for media placements.

The same holds true for a headshot. Find a local photographer who specializes in headshots. Anyone seeking media exposure needs a good headshot. This inexpensive investment will be worth its weight in gold.

MY FAVORITE TIP – Depending on your business, you might want to include some lifestyle shots of you in your business element and/or showing off your true personality.

Christina having fun with the camera in this lifestyle photo

TIP #9 – TRUSTWORTHINESS

*The glue that holds all relationships together ...
is trust, and trust is based on integrity.*
~ Brian Tracy

If your business doesn't appear to be trustworthy, it will be difficult to get good publicity. The good news is, a trustworthy business will have an easier time landing positive publicity.

The most important factor in gaining trust in the marketplace is providing a reliable service or product. Aside from that, by being consistent and accessible to your clients and customers, you'll gain an edge over most of the competition.

Your brand's story and values will be key factors in why people decide to trust it.

TIP #10 – THERE IS ONLY ONE BOSS

*Always do right.
This will gratify some people and astonish the rest.*
~ Mark Twain

It amazes me how many businesses don't understand customer service and how it affects their PR. In today's age of social media and online review sites, it is imperative to provide excellent customer service.

I manufacture hundreds of thousands of products and occasionally something isn't right. I've had rhinestones fall off or the petals of a daisy come apart. The few times we have received disappointing emails, we replied immediately, told the customer to throw it away, and sent a replacement out right away. They are usually astounded and profusely grateful with our response.

Do other businesses really not take care of their clients? Not only can an unhappy customer share their frustration with a potential customer in person, but they could also share it online through social media and reach thousands of people. Once that happens, you don't know what the ramifications might be to your business.

Always do the right thing with your customers!

MY FAVORITE TIP – When I owned the retail store, we told our employees we were a "yes" store and to treat our customers as such. We would bend over backwards to keep our customers happy and find anything they needed. We survived owning a "mom and pop" retail store in a blighted town, during an economic crash, because of our amazing customer service.

TIP #11 – WHAT FLOOR?

I'm sure you have heard the expression, "The Elevator Pitch." This narrative is a 30-second informational pitch about you, your company, or your product. You should be able to recite it freely as it could be something you have to do quickly with a journalist or someone interested in your company.

The concept of an elevator pitch is that if you had to tell someone about your company while riding in an elevator, how would you do it in that limited amount of time?

My elevator pitch is:

I'm Christina Daves, Founder of CastMedic Designs. We design and manufacture MediFashions, which are accessories to make walking medical boots fashion-forward, helping the injured look and heal their best and experience The Healing Power of Fashion®.

or

I'm Christina Daves, DIY Publicity Strategist and founder of PR for Anyone®. I help businesses use media to attract new customers and elevate their brand and authority to position them as an industry expert.

MY FAVORITE TIP – Liken your elevator pitch to a tweet. Get your message across briefly and to the point in 280 characters or less.

TIP #12 – KNOWLEDGE IS POWER

The best investment you can make is an investment in yourself.
The more you learn, the more you'll earn.
~ Warren Buffett

If you want to be *the* expert who is quoted on your topic, you should be able to talk about it effortlessly. Even if you think you know everything there is to know, learn more. In this book, I share my personal experiences, but I also went out and interviewed experts to make sure you could hear from them as well. Become the most knowledgeable person on your topic, present it well, and the media will come to you.

MY FAVORITE TIP – My grandmother, who was Jewish living in Berlin, Germany during WWII, used to always tell us to learn everything we could because no matter what happens in your life, no one can ever take knowledge away from you.

<u>**CASE STUDY**</u> – Je'net Kreitner founded Grandma's House of Hope, a non-profit in Orange County, California, that runs 14 housing units for the homeless. It would be difficult to land regular

media coverage for the facilities, however, positioning Je'net as an expert in homelessness has allowed her to gain regular media coverage that always refers back to her organization. This regular media exposure allows more people to learn about Grandma's House of Hope and the plight of the homeless in California. See Je'net on Today Show, www.PRforAnyone.com/GHHToday and on CBS in Los Angeles about cancer and the homeless, www.PRforAnyone.com/CBSLA.

TIP #13 – BE AUTHENTIC

The authentic self is the soul made visible.
~ Sarah Ban Breathnach

Nobody likes a phony. People want authenticity, now more than ever. When you are seeking publicity, or being interviewed, remember to stay true to yourself and your brand. Don't try to be something you're not. Being genuine and authentic will pay off in spades and should result in more interviews and more media coverage.

When I interviewed Natalie Mashaal, who got her producing start on the *Oprah Winfrey Show*, I specifically asked her how people such as, Dr. Oz, Dr. Phil, and Suze Orman became Oprah's go-to experts. She said it was their authenticity. They were real and believable, and the audience could relate to them.

TIP #14 – IT'S A WRAP

No matter what happens, always be yourself.
~ Dale Carnegie

Don't forget that it's your presence, your personality, and your overall brand that is the cornerstone of your PR efforts. Look professional, be consistent in your message, and be authentic and you'll be on your way to success!

Make a Name for Yourself

In life you are either the passenger or a pilot, it's your choice.
~ Anonymous

If you want to land media exposure, you're going to have to do some work and put yourself out there. It's unlikely the media is going to come banging on your door just because you've hung an "Open for Business" sign. That being said, there are things you can do to help stand out and be someone the media wants to feature.

This section provides you with ways to gain exposure for your business, leads you to new potential customers, and possibly helps you score some media coverage along the way. Whether you actually land media from these tips does not matter, as all of these ideas will help position you as an expert and influencer in your industry.

Please follow the tips in this book. I've seen the transformation that media can have on a business. There is no magic pill. You have to do the work. The good news, however, is that it's simple and once you start implementing it and seeing results, you're going to want to keep doing this in your business.

Ask yourself this question, "It's exactly one year from today. You have the same number of clients, the same number of leads, the same number of people on your list. Are you happy with where you are?" If you want to make a change this year, start implementing these tips and make landing publicity a regular part of your marketing.

TIP #15 – SHOUT IT FROM THE ROOFTOPS

If you are comfortable with it, and not everyone is, a great way to gain exposure is to speak. Come up with a topic or workshop idea, then sign up with local chambers of commerce and business networking groups. Speaking is also a great way to gain exposure to potential customers. My number one source of revenue is by acquiring clients from speaking engagements.

Often, there are members of the press covering these events, so there is the potential for them to cover your business too. I was asked to speak at a women's forum for our local chamber of commerce, and a few days later my name popped up in Google Alerts (more on this in Tip #22 below). A newspaper reporter wrote about the event and used a photograph of me speaking along with my name in the photo caption of the article.

Christina Daves shares her journey from having a great idea to getting her product to market. Her discussion was the keynote address at the Prince William Chamber Women's Forum Luncheon.

Featured in the Prince William Times for speaking at an event

As you continue to speak and gain experience and credibility, you will be able to apply for speaking at larger, national events, and of course there is more opportunity for national media exposure in that arena.

Both Toastmasters, www.Toastmasters.org and National Speakers Association, www.NSASpeaker.org are organizations to assist you with public speaking and there are many Speakers Bureaus who might be looking for your specific topic to add to their list of speakers.

MY FAVORITE TIP – My mentor, Peter, used to always tell me I needed to start speaking and share my story. I was petrified. I had never even taken public speaking in college. Every time we met, he said the same thing and I kept brushing the subject aside. One day Peter texted me to see if I was free on Wednesday at noon. I of course thought this was for our regular lunch meeting, so I said, "Yes." He replied with, "Good. I just backed out of a speaking engagement and put you in my place. Don't worry. It's a small group. You'll be fine." My stomach did a flip. How in the world was I going to speak to a group in a few days?

Peter knew I wouldn't let him down. I prepared something that included a page of notes from which I read almost the entire presentation. This was my sink or swim moment and at the end, I was shocked. Everyone loved it. They loved what I had done and my story of persistence. Peter was right. I hired coaches to learn how to speak with a purpose, and that was the start of my speaking career. I now speak on stages all across the country to thousands of people every year.

CASE STUDY – Jeff was a speaker at a Global Marketing event in California. Two weeks before he attended the event, he pitched the local media a segment idea involving his topic of personal brand. He landed this segment on his local ABC, www.PRforAnyone.com/ABCCA.

TIP #16 – ALWAYS PROVIDE VALUE FIRST

Influence is providing attention and value to others
~ Laura Fitton

I am a firm believer in Karma and the Universe returning good deeds. When you provide value first, the rest will take care of itself.

One of my first television appearances was on FOX5 in Washington, D.C. I definitely clicked with the news anchor and learned she liked entrepreneurial stories and particularly those involving women. Because of my connections in the entrepreneurial space, I was able to provide her many leads on great stories. These stories did not involve me as the expert, but they did allow me to stay front of mind with her for stories on which I could provide value.

One day she reached out to me because she had been offered to host a program about taking an invention from napkin to store shelves. The show was syndicated on FOX in over 30 markets across the United States. Guess who she chose to be her featured inventor? Me! Watch the segment here, www.PRforAnyone.com/FOXNational.

Serving as the featured inventor on The Next Great Thing television show syndicated across the U.S.

TIP #17 – THE GIVING TREE

No one has ever become poor by giving.
~ Anne Frank

Linking your business to a charity or a worthy cause is always a great way to generate publicity. Not only are you helping a cause you believe in, but hosting a charity event, donating a portion of the proceeds of sales, or donating product or services to a charity can be a positive PR coup as well. It puts you in a good light in the eyes of your customers, and there is always the possibility of media coverage.

The other thing to consider is the potential customers who believe in your cause and want to work with you because you have similar values.

I am a firm believer in giving back. Please don't give to charity just to try to gain publicity. In the long run, the good deed will do more for your PR than any media exposure you might get out of it, and you will feel good about giving back.

EXPERT TIP – According to a recent survey by Nielsen, more than half of global consumers are willing to pay more for goods and services from a company that gives back to society.

<u>**CASE STUDIES**</u> – Gail Romansky was featured in *Real Producers Magazine*. She is a real estate agent who lost a son to suicide. She is incredibly passionate about suicide prevention and hosts an annual walk. She was able to land this feature because of how she gives back to this community.

Gail Romansky featured in a magazine for her philanthropy

L.Y. Marlow founded Saving Promise to stop domestic violence that has plagued the women in her family for five generations. Her granddaughter's name is Promise and when she experienced abuse, L.Y. knew it had to stop. She created this non-profit to educate and create prevention programs in schools, workplaces, and the community. L.Y. pitched her local ABC station the day after we met and secured a segment date booked for October, which is National Domestic Violence Awareness month. Watch the segment at www.PRforAnyone.com/SavingPromise.

TIP #18 – AND THE WINNER IS....

Do not wait to strike till the iron is hot;
but make it hot by striking.
~ William B. Sprague

Look for awards and contests for which you can apply. Participating in and winning anything is a great opportunity for PR. There are tons of contests for new businesses, new products, websites, social media influencers, "Best of's," just about anything you can imagine. And with the Internet, they are easy to find. Don't forget to search locally too. Winning a local award is great for more local exposure.

Check your local chambers of commerce, local and national business groups, and local and national publications for any awards they host. Google is a great resource to find awards. Even if you see a contest or award that has been given already, set it up in your online alerts, and you'll be notified when it opens for the following year.

My first year in business, I was named one of the "Top 200 Leading Moms in Business" by StartupNation. I didn't win, but I was recognized and gained the benefits that came with their promotion of the award.

CASE STUDY - I was named *Entrepreneurial Rule Breaker of the Year* sponsored by Microsoft. This was a tremendous award and allowed me to gain massive exposure through Microsoft's network as well as other sponsors of the event, www.PRforAnyone.com/Rulebreaker.

Being interviewed across the globe after being named Entrepreneurial Rule Breaker of the Year

MY FAVORITE TIP – One of my Google Alerts is set for "product contest," another for "business award." This way, I receive notifications when pertinent contests or awards are announced.

TIP #19 – THE AWARD GOES TO...

Not only can you apply for an award, you can also create an award or scholarship that your company can hand out every year. It can be a small scholarship for a student-athlete or an award to a person in your community making a difference. You should be able to generate local buzz for giving this type of award. Even though it will be the recipient who is covered, you will gain peripheral media coverage as well.

CASE STUDY – Laura McGee is a real estate agent who lives in the town where Lydia Taft was the first woman to legally vote for President of the United States. Not only was she able to secure a local holiday for Lydia Taft Day, she also held an essay contest for local high school students about what it meant to live in this town during a time when a woman was then running for President. She landed quite a bit of media coverage including this popular real estate radio show on CBS in Boston. Laura used a contest not directly related to her business to secure media coverage that mentioned and linked back to her real estate business.

Laura McGee featured on CBS Radio in Boston

TIP #20 – IT'S PARTYTIME

Can you launch your business or product with an event and invite the media to attend? Keep in mind that an event could end up being quite costly, so there are probably much better ways to invest your start-up funds. If, however, you have the contacts or can work with someone in a collaborative effort, a unique event could be a way to gain exposure. Don't forget to invite the media using the tools we'll discuss later in the book.

MY FAVORITE TIP – When we opened *Details for the Home*, we worked with our town Mayor's office to host a ribbon-cutting ceremony. They invited other local dignitaries and notified the press, and we were covered in all of our local newspapers.

Ribbon cutting ceremony with the Mayor of Haymarket, VA

EXPERT TIP – The editor of my local newspaper gave me a great piece of advice for these types of events. He said, "If it's a grand opening of a Cupcakery, don't show the ribbon cutting, show the mayor taking a big bite of the cupcake." They want things that are different and creative. Think outside of the box when pitching the media.

TIP #21 – GET A FREE RIDE

Talk to your local university and see if there is an undergraduate or graduate public relations course and if they would be willing to use your business as a class or individual project.

I submitted CastMedic Designs as a potential project for graduate students at Trinity University in Washington, D.C. We were chosen, and one of the students prepared a wonderful campaign that involved Children's Hospital. It was something which I hadn't thought of and full of great ideas. Personally, I love working with both high school and college students because they have such fresh, creative minds and are so eager to learn and impress.

TIP #22 – ALERT!

Did you know that there are free services that allow you to set alerts online which can help you gain more publicity? These include: Google Alerts at www.Google.com/alerts, Mention at en.Mention.net, and Talkwalker at www.TalkWalker.com/alerts.

These are online services that search the Web to see if you or your business has been mentioned (see next tip for clipping services).

They allow you to monitor anything on the Web, then send you an email as soon as something for which you set an alert appears in their search results.

Everyone should be using one or all of these services to keep track of what is being said about them online. They are easy and free, and the results are incredible.

Some basics alerts you should have set up are:

- ❖ Your name
- ❖ Your business name

- ❖ Your business competitors
- ❖ The topic of your business
- ❖ Your key business words

If you have a common name such as John Smith, you'll need to add another search term that makes it unique, or you'll be receiving thousands of results for every John Smith in the world. Try John Smith and your business name or John Smith and your city.

For my business, if I can get a celebrity to wear my product, it's amazing PR.

One of my most successful Google Alerts has been "celebrity broken foot." The Paparazzi doesn't have anything on Google and me!

This alert has resulted in my finding several celebrities in medical boots to whom I reached out and inspired to make their medical boot fashionable, including Demi Lovato, Diana Ross, Carla Hall, Savannah Guthrie, and Olympic Gold Medalist, Jordyn Wieber, as well as several local news anchors and a host from QVC.

Carla Hall, Host of The Chew wears CastMedic Designs on the show

MAKE A NAME FOR YOURSELF · 31

Darci Strickland of WLTX in South Carolina sporting MediFashions onset

Another way to use these alerts is to build relationships with journalists. You can find out who is writing about your expertise. Then reach out to them by sharing and/or commenting on their articles or offering your services for future stories.

If you are an author of a specific topic that a journalist covers, ask them if they would be interested in a copy of your book.

TIP #23 – WHO'S TALKING ABOUT YOU?

Press clipping services, also known as media monitoring, are a way for businesses to track media coverage and determine what's being said about them and their competitors. It's similar to Google Alerts, Mention, and Talkwalker, but on a grander scale, and includes television, radio, newspapers, magazines, and social media. Google doesn't always index trade publications, small newspapers, or regional online sources, so there is limited information on where and when your company is being mentioned.

While media monitoring services can be more accurate than using Google and the others, they are not free, and can be quite costly depending on the level of service provided.

I recommend starting at these sites to determine if one is right for you:

Burrelles Luce, www.BurrellesLuce.com

Cision, https://www.Cision.com/us/products/monitoring/

Different services offer different levels of monitoring, so these are just a few examples of what's available.

TIP #24 – YOUR FOOTPRINT IN THE SAND

Why do you want publicity? At the end of the day, besides the visibility and credibility it provides, it's growing your digital footprint that really matters. It's likely that anyone who is considering working with you or any media outlet thinking of using you as a source is going to put your name into "Google" and see what comes up before they engage with you. Do you check out?

When you appear in top ranking media outlets, you get to borrow their "Google Juice" and appear higher in search rankings than from your own content. I call this riding the media's coattails. Enjoy the benefits of other people's higher rankings and make yourself look like the Rockstar you are.

Several years ago, if you put "Christina Daves" into Google, Christina Aguilera came up. She owned Google search results for our first name, Christina. After investing time into growing my digital footprint through media, now when you put my name into Google, I appear on over ten pages in Google.

MY FAVORITE TIP – I had an idea of partnering with one of my local credit unions. It is a $40 billion institution. As I'm sure you've gathered from this book so far, I'll try anything, and I'm not afraid to ask people for collaboration or ask the media for coverage. I sent an email to the president of this company on a Monday and he replied a few hours later asking if I could be in his office on Friday. When I arrived, I sat in his top floor office alone for a few minutes overlooking the gorgeous view of Washington, D.C. Suddenly, he came marching in and said, "Do you know what happens when you Google you?" I got that appointment because I checked out when he checked me out. He wanted to know who this woman was living in his backyard and wanted to hear more about my ideas of working together.

Get PR Famous Formula

You've got something really important and newsworthy to share with the world about you, your company or something you've accomplished. How do you share the news? Follow my proprietary system, the Get PR Famous Formula, to consistently land media coverage.

It's a simple 3-step process: you need to be newsworthy, you need to create great hooks, and you need to find the *right* journalist. Let's say you have a newsworthy story idea and a great hook to draw the journalist in, but you're pitching your business story to the beauty editor, it's falling on deaf ears. It is extremely unlikely that the beauty editor is going to forward your email to the business editor. People in the media are very busy themselves and they just don't have time to do something like that for you.

Let's say you've got a great newsworthy story idea, and you have the right journalist, but your hook, or your subject line, is boring with no "WOW" factor, there's a really good chance that your email will never get read. Maybe you can write a great hook and you've got the right journalist, but your story isn't newsworthy at all. You've basically wasted the journalist's time by opening the email. First of all, they're going to delete it because it isn't good, and second of all, you may have burned your bridge; and if they see a future email from you, they might just delete it before they even read it.

Follow these three steps and you will be light-years ahead of your competition when it comes to landing media coverage.

[Triangle diagram labeled "GET PR FAMOUS" with sides: "Be Newsworthy", "Create Great Hooks", "Find The Right Journalist"]

TIP #25 – PAID VS. EARNED

Publicity is absolutely critical. A good PR story is infinitely more effective than a front-page ad.
~ Richard Branson

To start, PR and advertising are not the same thing.

Advertising is something for which you pay. Because of that, you get to control the message. You are paying to tell people what you want them to hear. There is often less credibility with advertising because the audience knows you paid for it.

PR is free, but you don't get to control what someone else says about you. You provide information in an email or an interview. Then, you wait to see what someone else has to say about you. The upside to PR, besides being free, is that it creates instant authority. It's not you talking about you, it's someone else talking about you, which makes it more credible. PR is essentially a third-party endorsement of you or your company, otherwise known in the public relations industry as "earned media."

The potential downside is a journalist who doesn't see things the way you do and writes something not favorable. That actually happened to me very early on. A top blog site wrote about my products but didn't like them and said I had, "Tween-meets-Michaels" designs. Ouch! Kick in the stomach with that review. Ironically, that post has led to thousands of dollars in sales. (Thank you to Google Analytics for showing where sales are generated.) And the good news is, that is the only bad review I've ever received.

MY FAVORITE TIP - According to Nielsen, 92% of consumers around the world say they trust earned media above all other forms of advertising and recommendations.

TIP #26 – FOR IMMEDIATE RELEASE

I'm going to rattle a lot of heads here but my advice on the press release is, don't do it. The days of a press release carrying exclusivity and being seen by an elite few are gone. There are almost a million press releases sent out every year so having the journalist you want find your release is like finding a needle in a haystack. They are also very expensive to send. I recommend sticking to targeted pitching by finding the right journalist and sending them a good, newsworthy story idea.

There are times, however, when a press release might be advantageous to your particular business. It's up to you to decide when a posted press release outweighs cost and time. I have a client who is a woman-owned Government contractor and it is valuable for them to show when they win contracts. It's not picked up by the news, but it is posted online by a credible source and that is valuable to their business.

TIP #27 – ACTION!

If a picture is worth a thousand words, then a video is priceless.
~ Anonymous

When I shot my first video, it was truly awful! I had to submit a video with a funding application, so I sat in front of my laptop, taped sticky notes all around the screen, and tried to look and sound comfortable. It was so bad it's no wonder I never heard back from anyone!

I knew it was an important aspect of my business, so I just kept practicing. It became muscle memory and I'm pretty good at it now. I have been fortunate to interview some very prominent people, including Hoda Kotb, anchor of the *Today Show*, the Features Editor of *Parade Magazine*, *New York Times* bestselling authors, and more. I also have a regular segment on *Good Morning Washington*. Now, I absolutely love being on camera. I do keep that original video on my computer to remind myself of how easy it is to conquer obstacles and improve.

Video is vital for a business. 90% of all content consumed online is through video. Posting a video online allows people to learn about and get to know you. They also have the ability to share it on their social networks and it gives the news media and bloggers something to repost and/or use. Don't get lost by being in the 10%.

Video is a great way to assist in search engine optimization (SEO) by using keywords in the title and tagging those words when you upload the video to a free hosting service such as YouTube or Vimeo. If the video is repeatedly shared on other sites, it continues to build links to your website and assists in strengthening your search engine optimization (SEO).

If you find you are uncomfortable in front of the camera, just keep practicing. You will get better and better at it. I promise. If I could make this shift from absolutely awful videos to now regularly appearing on television, you can too.

MY FAVORITE TIP – Most iPads now have a built-in teleprompter. Type in your script, set the speed, and you're all set.

TIP #28 – PITCH PERFECT

Don't forget to proofread, proofread, proofread. These are, after all, journalists. Make sure the entire media pitch is free from grammatical and typographical errors and that all the links work correctly. Double-check statistics and facts. In some instances, a journalist might just print your entire email, or portions thereof, so it is critical that what you send out is perfect.

TIP #29 – WHO CARES?

Who is your target audience? Who would want to know about your newsworthy story? All media outlets share their demographics online so make sure you are targeting the right outlet for your message.

Start building a list of specific media outlets such as television shows, news programs, radio shows, magazines, newspapers, podcasts and blogs that report on your topic. These contacts are the ones you should approach with a targeted story idea.

TIP #30 – MAKE YOUR MARK

*"You can't wait for inspiration;
you have to go after it with a club."*
~ Jack London

A targeted story idea is one that is personalized for the format of a television or radio show, or a magazine or newspaper. It is very important to know the show or publication before you send a targeted story idea. Do your homework and pitch something you know they are going to want to cover in their media outlet.

The media is always looking for fresh ideas, so if you've got something, send it in. I recommend doing it via email as that seems to be the preferred medium of journalists.

Remember that the media are inundated with email, so yours needs to stand out. I heard a *CNBC* journalist say he receives anywhere from 500 to 1,000 emails per day. Don't send a lengthy email. Make it easy for them.

This is the formula we use that works well:

Segment Idea: Catchy Title—See TIP #47—The Art of the Hook

Talking Points: Provide a bulleted list of 3-5 talking points (add a statistic or quote if relevant)

Visuals: Media loves visuals

Experience: Mention if you have media experience and put a link to a press kit or website showing prior media experience

Photos: Head Shot/Product Shot/Book Cover

Contact Information: Name, email, and phone number

Short Bio: 2-3 sentences on your expertise

TIP #31 – PAPARAZZI

Visuals are a critical component in today's quest for media. Always send low-resolution photos and let the media know that high-resolution photos are available. You don't want to clog up or delay their email inbox with huge image files.

TIP #32 – COME BEARING GIFTS

If you think you would be better served having a reporter or editor touch and feel your product or learn about your business firsthand, you could opt to send the traditional press kit. A press kit contains your one-sheet, bio, photos, and samples.

Whatever you're sending, whether an envelope or a package, make yourself stand out. Use bright colored envelopes and folders. Use big type on the envelope. If you are sending product, be creative.

I learned this lesson the hard way. I went to New York City with a friend and designated one day of our trip to be my big PR campaign stop. I made about fifteen packets in manila folders and headed to the main offices of all the major magazines on Avenue of the Americas. I walked into the main lobby, fully confident, went right up to the receptionist and said, "I have a package to drop off for Ms. Editor of *Fashion Magazine*."

They directed me to the mailroom, which is a room located outside the building around the corner of the main building. I walked in, and I am not kidding when I tell you that the entire mail reception desk was five deep with gorgeous colorful bags with silk ribbons and stunning wrapped boxes as well as branded packages accessorized with tulle and balloons. My heart sank as I looked down at my manila envelopes. I left them, but realized they might not even get past the mail clerk downstairs, who would probably select and deliver all the pretty packages first. Not surprisingly, I didn't hear back from anyone after those deliveries.

I caution against sending a lot of product or items that are costly without a journalist knowing they are coming. I have a colleague who mailed over $1,500 worth of product to a television producer who never received them. The mailroom is a busy area at a media outlet, so it's important to be very specific to whom you mail and what you are sending.

Be unique. Be different. As I continue to say, "Think outside of the box." One thing that continues to get me noticed is the delicious custom cookies I have made by a local specialty baker. They are designed as medical boots decorated in a leopard Sock-It, one of my products.

Custom cookies decorated as medical boots with a leopard Sock-It

TIP #33 – COLLABORATE

*No person will make a great business who
wants to do it all himself or get all the credit.*
~ Andrew Carnegie

Come up with a good way to present your ideas, especially if you are a product-based business. Products are difficult to place by themselves and most magazines won't write about one specific product. You will stand a much better chance of placing your story if it relates to a bigger picture theme or topic.

Don't be afraid to collaborate with other people. My first appearance on my local *FOX* station was pitching my product, along with others for "National Healthy Foot Month." I was one of several products being featured on that segment.

MY FAVORITE TIP – My client Connie invented a product called, Tip 'n Split **which is a calculator for instantly figuring out the tip and how to divvy up a restaurant bill. Her ideal customer is over 55 years old; so she was very targeted when she pitched the media and put Tip 'n Split in product roundups. In one year, Tip 'n Split appeared on the** *Today Show, Good Morning America, Real Simple Magazine, The View* **and many more. Here is her Today Show segment,** www.PRforAnyone.com/TipnSplitToday **and View Your Deal Segment on** *The View,* www.PRforAnyone.com/TheView.

TIP #34 – PRACTICE MAKES PERFECT

Have no fear of perfection, you'll never reach it.
~ Salvador Dali

When trying to gain media exposure, everyone wants to start with the golden crown of morning television, such as the *Today Show* or *Good Morning America*. It is, however, very unlikely for you to start on a show such as this. You first need to earn your wings and establish yourself as an expert on the local level.

If you are nervous right now just thinking about getting media exposure, imagine if your very first experience was on a nationally broadcast live morning show? If you bomb, that's it! There probably won't be a next time.

I'm not trying to scare you. I just want you to have realistic PR aspirations as a newbie. Remember, I landed everything I did in one year, so it doesn't have to take a long time. It's just important to get a few interviews under your belt first before going to the National level.

Make it Work for You

What is newsworthy? Newsworthy stories are timely, important and interesting. The benefit of providing good, newsworthy stories to the media is that they will cover you and when they do, you get to put their media logos on your website, which makes you more credible.

The other thing that this does is it builds your digital footprint. Before anyone works with you, they are going to Google you. Imagine if they put your name into Google and you appear on page after page filled with articles or television programs about your industry that names you. That is the power of media.

You just have to remember that media is 24/7/365. They need you. If you learn how to be newsworthy and how to give the media good story ideas, you will be someone who is regularly featured in the media.

In this section we go over various themes and topics to use to make your business newsworthy.

GET FAMOUS FORMULA

Be Newsworthy
Create Great Hooks
Find The Right Journalist

TIP #35 – HOW FAST CAN THIS GO?

Many of my clients have landed their first media appearance within thirty days of trying. That's how accurate this system is when it's implemented consistently. Some people have landed in the media within days of sending their pitch in. For others, it might take longer but isn't the end result worth the effort?

CASE STUDY – One of my very first clients was Jennifer Fugo of www.GlutenFreeSchool.com. By following the system and using tips found in this book, she landed not one, but two appearances on the *Dr. Oz* show in thirty days. She branded herself as the "Face of Gluten Sensitivity" and wrote a book about how to shop at the grocery store affordably when you have to restrict gluten from your diet.

These appearances put her on the map in the Gluten-Free space and positioned her as an authority in this industry. She is now asked to speak all over the country on topics related to gluten sensitivity.

MAKE IT WORK FOR YOU · 47

Jennifer Fugo of Gluten Free School appears on the Dr. Oz show

TIP #36 – TELL THE WORLD YOU'RE HERE!

Great things are done by a series of small things brought together."
~ Vincent van Gogh

First and foremost, let me re-emphasize *newsworthy*. Journalists are looking for story ideas their audience is going to *want* to learn about. Imagine yourself sitting on your front porch with a cup of coffee, reading the newspaper or a magazine. What is it that you would want to read about?

Some newsworthy topics could include:

- ❖ Launching a New Product
- ❖ Announcing a Contest
- ❖ Receiving or Giving an Award

- Representing Your Non-Profit
- A Grand Opening
- Tie-in a Trend
- Create Controversy
- Provide Tips
- Associate with Current Events
- Apply Seasonality
- Use Celebrity

Before you send anything out, ask yourself if you would be interested in hearing the story or learning more about the topic. If your answer is "yes", read on to learn various methods for sharing your story.

TIP #37 – GO BEYOND THE BOX

I've given you some ideas above, but the key is to think outside of and beyond the box. Don't pitch what everyone else is going to pitch. Stand out and be unique in your approach. One of my favorite things to do is take what is going on in the world and bring it home to your community. Use http://trends.google.com/ and www.Twitter.com to see what people are talking about. If it's trending online, the media knows about it and will be anxious to hear what you have to say.

TIP #38 – BE NEW-SWORTHY

Think left and think right and think low and think high.
Oh, the thinks you can think up if only you try!"
~ Dr. Seuss

New is what all journalists are looking for. They want the "scoop." They want to be the first to report on a new idea, new product, or new business. As busy as you might be right when you launch your business, don't forget to send out an initial announcement to applicable journalists, telling the world you are here. It is likely that you will gain some sort of media coverage just from announcing something new.

Don't worry if you aren't "new" anymore. Reinvent yourself by creating something new about your company. Do you have a new product? A big new client? Can you collaborate with someone on a new concept? Think creatively about how you can reinvent yourself or your business and create something *new* that can become *news*worthy.

I over-manufactured our MediFashions, so I had to recreate "new" for media coverage. One of my favorites was after I heard that camouflage was the new hot style for women. I took the male version of the Camouflage "Sock-It" and coupled it with a hot pink rhinestone "Strap-It" flower and announced our "new" design.

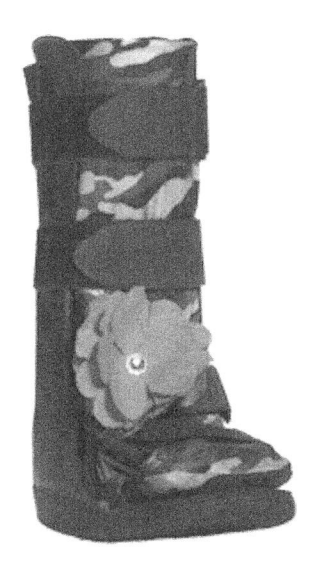

TIP #39 – NICHE THE PITCH

What are you doing differently than anyone else in your industry? Think of a target. Think of the outer rim as your main industry; the white circle is narrowing down your niche and then the red circle is what you do differently than anyone else. What is your red circle? This is what you use to land media coverage.

CASE STUDY – Shari Jaeger Goodwin is a Business Coach. She specializes in leadership coaching (white ring) and her red target is a program she hosts on her farm where she trains CEOs in leadership skills using her horses. She was featured on the cover of her local newspaper business section for this program.

Shari Goodwin Jaeger is featured on the front page of the Fauquier Times Business Section

TIP #40 – MEDIA BEGETS MEDIA

Exciting for Shari is that after this article ran, she was able to secure a spot on her local *FOX* television station sharing the same story. Once you have been covered by the media, it's as if you've been vetted by them as well, making it much easier to land the next article or television segment. See Shari's segment at www.PRforAnyone.com/ShariOnFOX. All it takes is one media appearance to continue getting additional coverage for your business.

TIP #41 – SEASONALITY

Whether it is Winter, Spring, Summer, or Fall, there are always news stories related to the seasons. What can you pitch the media that relates to your expertise at a certain time of year? You can also borrow stories from other areas of the country or world, even if it's not happening where you are. Entice the media by saying, "If this happened here…"

<u>CASE STUDY</u> – Patricia is a travel agent. She was featured on her local CBS morning show talking about what happens when a hurricane hits an island to which you are supposed to be traveling. She talked about travel strategies and as you can see, her name and company were featured in the story. This ended up being an almost six-minute segment featuring her as the travel expert. Watch her story at, www.PRforAnyone.com/Travel.

TIP #42 – DAVID VS. GOLIATH

Is there something going on in your industry by a large player that you disagree with? The media loves a David vs. Goliath story. Are you David? Agreeing with everything isn't something that is newsworthy, but if you take on a well-known entity and can provide a strong point, the media will be interested in your story.

CASE STUDY - One of my clients, Pat, who is a real estate agent and often works as a Buyer's Agent was very upset when Redfin announced they would no longer represent buyers. I helped her formulate her pitch and she sent it in to the *Washington Post*. The next week, she was repeatedly quoted in a full-page article entitled, *Redfin's newest online tool cuts out the buyer's agent*. If a buyer is looking for representation and they see this article, who do you think they are going to want to use to represent them when they purchase their home?

TIP #43 – BE NON-TRADITIONAL

> *I want all my senses engaged.*
> *Let me absorb the world's variety and uniqueness.*
> *~ Maya Angelou*

Using non-traditional holidays is one of my favorite tools for pitching the media. These are unique holidays that have been established over time and can hopefully help spark creative ideas for submitting story ideas.

Use this calendar to help you think outside of the box and come up with unique story ideas to increase your chances of being covered in the media.

Some unique holidays include:

- ❖ Better Business Communication Day
- ❖ National Simplify Your Life Week
- ❖ Random Acts of Kindness Day
- ❖ Business Women's Day
- ❖ Customer Service Week
- ❖ National Relaxation Day

Come up with some creative ways to tell your story, in a non-traditional way, for a better chance of gaining coverage in the media.

CASE STUDIES I submitted a story about CastMedic Designs for National Healthy Foot Month in April and appeared on the local *FOX* news in Washington, D.C., www.PRforAnyone.com/HealthyFootMonth.

Additionally, a submission I sent in for National Inventors Month in May led to a story in the *Washington Post*.

A client's food product, Slawsa, was featured on the *Today Show* for National Hotdog Day. Watch at www.PRforAnyone.com/SlawsaonToday.

Slawsa is featured on the Today Show for National Hot Dog Day

TIP #44 – DO YOUR HOMEWORK

By failing to prepare, you are preparing to fail.
~ Benjamin Franklin

Spend time researching the media outlet in which you want to appear. How do they run stories? What format do they use? By doing this extra step and pitching what they want to see, you will increase your chance of success.

CASE STUDY – My client Matt wrote a book called *The A.D.D. Entrepreneur* about building and selling a multi-million-dollar car repair service while having severe attention deficit disorder. He was not able to hold meetings for more than two minutes at a time but still grew an incredibly successful business. In seeking media exposure, we found that a local ABC anchor, who hosts a business show, had been diagnosed with A.D.D. in her forties. This was the perfect tie-in for Matt's book and landing a television appearance.

Matt Curry is featured on ABC's Washington Business Report

TIP #45 – CELEBRITY SELLS

I see stardom very clearly as a construct that's been created in order to sell things.
~ Julie Christie

One day I saw an article about Diana Ross arriving in Los Angeles after breaking her foot while in Europe. The picture was of her in a wheelchair and a medical boot. I went on to read the story and it said that she would still be coming to Washington, D.C. in two weeks to sing for the President of the United States.

I jumped on the opportunity. I found her manager through a simple Google search. I was able to send him an email describing my product and how it would benefit her by being able to make her medical boot fashionable. He forwarded my email to Ms. Ross and said she wanted to wear something when she was in D.C. I was able to meet her staff at her hotel and leave products for her to choose from. The morning after her event, there were pictures all over the internet with Diana Ross wearing one of my flowers on her medical boot. This was a game-changer for my business. I was now able to benefit from the credibility of Diana Ross wearing my product.

Even if you have no connection to a celebrity, can you tie something they do or have done to your business?

CASE STUDY – My client Naomi, a real estate agent, listed Linda Hamilton of Terminator movie fame's farm in Virginia. She sent her pitch to the *Washington Post* who covered the story, www.washingtonpost.com/news/where-we-live/wp/2015/10/30/terminator-star-linda-hamilton-sells-leesburg-farm/ and then it was also picked up in many local publications. Not only did she sell Linda's property, she also got other business as a result of this article.

MAKE IT WORK FOR YOU · 57

TIP #46 – WHAT'S THE STORY?

Since I've shared some real estate case studies, I want to direct this one tip to agents. Do your homework on a property. Pay attention to any history, former owners, anything that has happened to the property or on the property that has significance. These are all newsworthy story ideas.

<u>CASE STUDY</u> – My client Tara got the listing of this beautiful home that was built in the 1800's. It was one of the original hotels outside of Washington, D.C. An interesting characteristic about that home was that it has a pint-sized bathroom. There is history about this in that homes built during that time only had restrooms on the upper floor in the bedrooms so guests would have to go through someone's bedroom to use the lavatory. This house had a small restroom built under the stairs, which at that time was called a pint-sized bathroom. There are only a handful of homes with these left in the country so that was the story angle.

WASHINGTONPOST.COM
Restoring this house in Burke, Va., was truly a labor of love
HOUSE OF THE WEEK | Damien Chaves rebuilt the circa 1898 home for...

Featured House of the Week in the Washington Post

TIP #47 – THE ART OF THE HOOK

The next step in the *Get PR Famous Formula* is Creating Great Hooks. The first thing anyone sees when looking at an email is the subject line. Whether they like it or not will determine whether they go any further in reading your story idea. It is vital to create a catchy headline that will stand out.

You won't get a second chance to make this first impression.

TIP #48 – COVER STORY

The best place to see hook examples is on a magazine's cover. People are paid to "hook" a potential purchaser into buying the magazine based on what's on the cover. Think of where we purchase magazines. They are in the grocery store check-out aisle. This is an impulse purchase based on what you read on the cover. Write your hooks as if you were trying to sell a magazine.

You can also Google magazine covers where you think you'd be a fit and see what types of hooks they use on the cover. Use that as a guideline when writing your hook. Give them what they want, and you'll have better results landing media coverage.

CASE STUDY – Dr. Cammi Balleck, a Doctor of Naturopathy who specializes in conditions of the thyroid, pitched, *Sure Cure for Wired & Tired*, to *First for Women Magazine* and not only did they do an article based on her story idea, they used her hook, *Sure Cure for Wired and Tired*, on the cover of the magazine.

TIP #49 – COMING UP NEXT...

Another way to get a feel of what a good hook is, is to watch what happens on television news shows before they go to break. They usually say something like, "Coming up next..." That teaser is a *hook* to get you to stay through the commercials to watch the next riveting story. Advertisers are who pay for the programming, so they want you to stay and watch what they are offering. One of my favorites was when my kids were still in school and had summer reading assigned. The hook was, "Coming up next, a book your kids will actually want to read this summer." Pay attention to these television hooks and you'll start to get ideas of how you can incorporate your business or story idea into a great hook.

TIP #50 – WHERE ARE YOU?

The last part of the formula is finding the right journalist. This is a critical part of the puzzle because you don't want to send your story pitch to someone who isn't going to care about it and will likely delete it. We are very fortunate to live in a time where the internet provides an incredible amount of data and resources. Finding the right journalist is a simple Google search: "who writes about x for y." If it doesn't come right up, you might have to get a little creative with your keywords, but it should not be a time-intensive exercise to find the right journalist.

We Want YOU!

Your uniqueness is your greatest strength,
not how well you emulate others.
~ Simon S. Tam

When the judge said, "*We pick* (long, dramatic pause…) *The Boot*!"

I was stunned! Did she really say that? "The Boot!" That was me—I had the boot. It meant they had picked me. I won!

At that moment, I knew exactly how Miss America or an Academy Award® winner feels when they say, "*I'm shocked! I really didn't expect to win.*"

Nobody plopped a giant tiara on my head or handed me a golden statue. Even better, I had just won $20,000 on the *Steve Harvey Show's* Top Inventor Competition for my medical boot fashion accessories!

Steve Harvey Show Top Inventor Competition

This moment of greatness stemmed from the three minutes it took me to respond to a producer's query.

You don't think it's that easy to gain media coverage? Think again, because it really is.

Reporters are looking for people like us to help them with their stories. They need sources and experts they can quote. Television and radio shows need guests every single day. And bloggers are always on the hunt for new information.

You can become an expert in the media for free. All you have to do is sign up for media query services (see below). They will send you daily emails from journalists about various topics being covered.

Respond regularly to these queries with good content and you will start to see consistent media coverage, while you build valuable relationships. It's really that easy.

Remember, it takes time. If you don't hear back right away, be patient. Continue to respond in a timely manner and always be on-topic. Allow time for the journalists to recognize your expertise and to start using you in stories. I had answered the query for the *Steve Harvey Show* in August. By the time I heard back in October, I had almost completely forgotten about it.

TIP #51 – HELP A REPORTER OUT

My favorite free service is Help a Reporter Out (HARO). They once told me I was one of their biggest success stories. I use it every day in my own business and regularly send queries to my private clients. The website is www.HelpaReporter.com. All you have to do is visit the site, sign up and—voila!—media queries will start appearing in your mailbox that day.

The basic service is completely free and is comprised of journalists looking for experts or people who can comment on topics about which they are writing.

During the week, three times a day (at around 6:00 a.m., 1:00 p.m., and 6:00 p.m., EST, excluding holidays) you will receive email queries from journalists who are looking for experts, quotes, and information on stories they are writing. You will even see queries from television producers looking for guests.

There are between twenty and forty queries each time and rarely is there a duplicate query throughout the day. I won't sugar-coat it; the emails are monotonous. It's just a list of sentences and there are a lot. That being said, would one media hit exposing you or your business to millions of potential customers be worth five minutes of monotony a day? I don't just think so, I know so!

When I mentioned my digital footprint earlier and how many pages of Google have "Christina Daves" on them, I can account much of that success to being quoted from HARO queries. Personally, I have appeared on *The Steve Harvey Show* and *Dr. Oz* and been quoted in *Forbes, Entrepreneur,* and *Success* Magazines as a direct result of responding to HARO queries. I've appeared in over 1,000 media outlets and many of those stem from HARO.

Go to www.FreeGiftfromChristina.com and get my cheat sheet for how to best respond to HARO queries with the likelihood of being covered.

EXPERT TIP – Professionalism is the #1 tip for pitching reporters on HARO. This tip may sound obvious, but we often hear from reporters that the pitches they receive are poorly written. A well-crafted pitch is free of slang, spelling mistakes, and grammatical errors. This shows the reporter that you mean business. Don't sacrifice quality and professionalism in order to respond quickly. Put your best foot forward and you'll immediately increase your chances of success. ~ Natalia Dykyj, Former VP, Product Management, Cision (HARO's parent company).

<u>**CASE STUDY**</u> – My client Cedric, used HARO to appear in Realtor.com 30 times in six months and he was also featured in an article

in *Women's Health* Magazine that has a circulation of close to 11 million readers. His consistent use of HARO has made him a real estate Rockstar and helped him win listings because of his authority and credibility.

Women'sHealth   HEALTH   FITNESS   GET ABS –NO GYM REQUIRED   WEIGHT LOSS   SUBSCRIBE

The 3 Relationship Red Flags That Only Your Realtor Might Notice
"Stress management is crucial in love and in real estate."

BY JAMIE HERGENRADER October 11, 2017

Realtor says: "Thirteen years in this business has given me insight into how people handle stress," says Cedric Stewart, residential and commercial sales consultant at Keller Williams Realty in Washington D.C. "When I've had to tell couples their dream home will exceed their budget, some will talk it through together, unlike others who say, 'Well, you're the one who wanted that extra bedroom.' Let's just say I've had to resell a few houses for those couples. Stress management is crucial in love and in real estate."

TIP #52 – PITCHRATE

PitchRate is very similar to HARO. What I like about PitchRate is that you can insert a photo which is a feature not available on HARO.

According to their founding company, Wasabi Communications, "PitchRate.com is a free media matchmaking service providing a powerful tool for journalists looking for sources, and giving experts media coverage opportunities."

Sign up at www.PitchRate.com

EXPERT TIP – If you see a media request that speaks to you, don't wait. Make a pitch right away! Once a journalist gets what they need, they may "turn off" their request even if the deadline hasn't been reached. And remember, only respond to requests you can speak about. Irrelevant pitches are considered noise by journalists. Keep your pitches short, simple and concise. ~ Hannah Colson, Pitch Rate.

TIP #53 – SOURCE BOTTLE

Source Bottle is located in Australia and according to their website, "has journalists from the United States, Canada, UK and Ireland, and New Zealand" as well. Their service is free.

As with the other services, you receive an email with various media queries. Within one week of signing up, I had three media "hits" from Source Bottle, one of which was a national publication.

Sign up at: www.sourcebottle.com.

TIP #54 – QWOTED

I recently learned about Qwoted and signed up right away. If you are in the financial space, Qwoted is a must! They started out as a query service in the financial space but are expanding their categories. I was already quoted as a PR expert for *FOX Business*. The other benefit about Qwoted is their database of reporters that you can access at no charge and gain all of their contact information and social media handles.

CASE STUDY - In the first week of signing up for Qwoted, I was quoted in *FOX Business* about a story on Oprah's national tour, https://www.foxbusiness.com/media/oprah-winfrey-weight-watchers-tour-heres-what-experts-say

TIP #55 – JOURNOREQUESTS

If you're based in Europe or specifically the United Kingdom, check out Journorequests. It's very similar to HARO and Source Bottle but the majority of their queries are based in Europe.

Check it out at: http://www.journorequests.com/

TIP #56 – DON'T BE LATE

> *The early bird gets the worm.*
> *~ Norman Ralph Augustine*

When you find a query that piques your interest, one of the most important ways of attracting attention is to be timely in your response. HARO, for example, has a huge database, so a reporter may receive hundreds of responses to one query. If the reporter gets a good response right away, anything that comes in afterwards might be disregarded. The best thing you can do is to respond to a pertinent query as soon as possible.

Not sure it's worth it? My clients have used these free media query sites and appeared in the *Wall Street Journal, U.S. News and World Report, Psychology Today, Bloomberg, Dr. Oz, Women's Health Magazine*, local affiliates of ABC, NBC, CBS, and FOX and many more, exposing their product, service or brand to millions of potential customers.

The media is going to use someone in their story, make sure it's you.

TIP #57 – DON'T GO "FISHING"

*One of the most sincere forms of respect is
actually listening to what another has to say.*
~ Bryant McGill

Do not respond off-topic. Even if the media outlet making the request is one you have been trying to reach through other avenues. Yes, the email will get to them, but they will not be happy that your email has nothing to do with what they are working on at that moment. These journalists are usually up against fast approaching deadlines, so it is a waste of their resources to read responses not pertinent to their query.

With HARO, responding with unrelated information is in fact against their policies, and you could be banned from the site if you violate this policy.

MY FAVORITE TIP – Be respectful of the reporter's time!

TIP #58 – K.I.S.S

Simplicity is the glory of expression.
~ Walt Whitman

Reporters don't have time to read lengthy emails. Make your response easy to scan and read. Use bullets if possible and bold important words. Be brief. Some of my biggest successes have come from two-sentence responses.

Provide your contact info. They will get back to you if there is a fit. And I stress this point, do not forget to provide your contact information.

In an interview I conducted with a product manager of HARO, she said I would be shocked at how many people forget to include any contact information. If journalists don't know who you are, they can't contact you.

Lastly, remember how many responses these journalists receive, and don't get frustrated if you don't hear back.

They could have opened one email and found that source to be perfect. The story could have gotten shelved. Or, for example, in the case of my appearance on the Steve Harvey Show, I responded to that query in August and didn't hear back for two months.

Responding to the queries is something you have to commit to diligently. If you do, you will get results.

MY FAVORITE TIP – One of the things I hear over and over is, "I don't have time to answer these queries!" A time-saving tip that I use, is to save specific boilerplate responses I can use for various topics. Because they are already written out and need just a little tweaking, I can create a response to a query in no time. I have sample response emails for queries related to product pitches, business expert, "Mompreneur," start-ups, radio guest, television guest, etc., that require only minor edits. This system allows me to quickly respond to queries on various topics.

TIP #59 – BE KIND

No act of kindness, no matter how small, is ever wasted.
~ Aesop

If possible, always personalize your queries. Most journalists' names will appear in the query. Go the extra step to address your response directly to the journalist with "Dear (Name)."

TIP #60 – NO PHOTOS PLEASE

Do not include images with HARO. Their response system strips images. When you respond to a HARO query and want to include an image, you will have to do that via a link to your website. Queries will often ask for images, but you still have to link versus inserting an image. Some queries looking for images will include a personal email address versus the query address. In that case, you may respond to their personal email address and attach images.

TIP #61 – TWEET, TWEET

Twitter is also a great place to find journalists who use the query services. If you see something pertinent, tweet at the journalist. With only 280 characters, your reply needs to be clear and concise. It's great practice to respond to these types of queries.

- ❖ Follow HARO at twitter.com/helpareporter, @helpareporter. HARO posts many of their queries on Twitter and they also provide great tips for accessing journalists and how to respond properly.

- ❖ If you see #UrgHARO in the tweet, it means a journalist is urgently seeking a source. I often do a quick #UrgHARO search to see if there is anything to which I can respond.

- ❖ Follow PitchRate at @PitchRate, twitter.com/pitchrate. They have several urgent queries throughout the day and also provide various tips.

- ❖ Follow SourceBottle at @SourceBottle, twitter.com/sourcebottle. Their Twitter feed is full of media requests.

- Follow Qwoted at @Qwoted, twitter.com/qwoted. They put their media requests here as well.

Another little trick is to search "#journorequest" on Twitter to see what journalists are looking for.

TAKE IT AWAY

It is in your moments of decision that your destiny is shaped.
~ Tony Robbins

Important take-aways from this section are:

1) Set up boilerplate responses to various queries. You'll basically create your boilerplate responses as you answer new queries. I save mine in a separate email folder so, when a similar query comes in, I copy and paste the content and just edit the name and any specifics.
2) Sign up for the media query services and connect with them on their various social media platforms.
3) Always include your contact information.

The Road to Stardom

The important thing is somehow to begin.
~ Henry Moore

We were sitting in Panera Bread in the middle of our interview when the reporter asked me, "Why haven't you submitted this story before? This is so great!" I looked at her dumbfounded. I live in the Washington D.C. area. I've submitted story ideas to the *Washington Post* over and over again, but this was the first time a reporter responded. That's when she gave me the scoop on how things really work in the back room of newspapers. I've come to find the same holds true with local television too.

When you send an email to the general email box of a media outlet, it could be any one of a number of reporters or producers who sees it. You never know who might like the idea and who won't. Just because one person passes on it doesn't mean it won't eventually get covered.

I sent in a story idea for National Inventors Month in May that happened to catch this reporter's eye. I submitted my product various ways to the *Post* the year prior, but I didn't get any bites. She had never seen any of my story ideas before. She happened to notice this one and contacted me for the interview.

It was my persistence that landed a story about my business in the *Washington Post*. I kept developing new angles and finally found the right connection.

In this section, I'll share other tips to help you increase your chances of being covered in a newspaper or magazine.

TIP #62 – ARE YOU THE ONE?

You will never influence the world by being just like it.
~ Sean McCabe

Is there a particular magazine in which you see yourself, your business, or your product? Make sure you know who reads the magazine and that your topic or story resonates with them and also fits the style of the magazine. Your goal is to provide value to their audience.

This research can easily be done on Google by searching the publication name and the word "demographics." If you see a fit, either buy a copy of it or visit your local library and read the entire magazine.

Read the magazine as if you had written it, versus reading it for pleasure.

Try to gain the perspective of the magazine and what they are trying to portray to their readers.

Ask yourself:

- What content or topics area featured in the magazine?
- To whom are they writing?
- What is the feel of the magazine?
- Do you easily visualize your product, story, or business in that publication?
- Is there a particular section in which your story fits?

If you can answer these questions and they pertain to you or your business, then it's time to formulate your story idea.

The same holds true for a newspaper, but it's really about what section you fit? Metro or Local? Lifestyle? Travel? Business?

Now that you've decided on the publication and the section, it's time to write a great story idea.

TIP #63 – MAKE IT EPIC!

> *Do not go where the path may lead,*
> *go instead where there is no path and leave a trail.*
> *~ Ralph Waldo Emerson*

The key to PR is having a great story to tell. Nobody likes a boring story. Make your story exciting or interesting. Share something you would want to know about.

A popular method of submitting to a magazine or newspaper is to provide a list of ideas or tips.

For example:

- ❖ An interior designer might submit: 5 Tips for Decorating a Dorm Room for Under $50

- ❖ A Realtor® might submit: The Top 3 "Bang-for-your-Buck" Upgrades to Sell Your House

- ❖ A relationship expert might submit: *7 Ways to "X" Your Ex!*

Take your expertise and turn it into a list with a really great headline and hook.

Another popular story idea is one that is alarming. For example, a story idea I submitted with great success was "WARNING: Kids Might Want to Break Their Foot to Wear This."

Can you cause controversy with your topic? This concept is another great way to get coverage. My friend, Bryan Toder, The No

Fear Guy, www.thenofearzone.com, gets quite a bit of exposure with his story idea of: *Nicotine is not an addiction and I can prove it by asking you one simple question.* You're hooked, right? You want to know *what* is that question.

What's your story? Do you have something compelling you can share? Why did you start your business? What's the human element you can share about your story that would engage readers?

As for formatting your story idea: make it concise, on target, and easy to read. Include a visual if possible. If there are statistics to back your story, use them. Always make sure you show the editor why he or she should cover this story. Show them how it benefits their audience.

EXPERT TIP – Be radically helpful to your editor! Put yourself in her shoes. Think the way she thinks. What problem does she have that you could solve? What do her readers want and need? Put a ton of value in that first contact, and you'll be really well positioned for that coveted call back. ~ Gay Edelman, Former Senior Editor, Family Circle Magazine, Writing Coach, www.coachgay.com.

TIP #64 – WHAT'S NEWSWORTHY WHEN?

In general, the calendar year is broken down into certain topics the media covers. Try to gear your story ideas to these seasonable trends.

The first quarter of the calendar year is geared towards New Year's resolutions. Many stories and articles are about weight loss and fitness and how to reach those goals as well as getting organized in the New Year.

The second quarter is geared towards summer: travel, fashion, and summer fun.

The third quarter is a very slow news time and many reporters are very accessible. This time of year is great to present a new product or service. Also, if you have anything pertinent for Back-to-School, submit it at this time. Note: August is the slowest news month and the easiest time to get publicity.

The end of the year is the biggest news time with everyone reflecting back on the year, so it's very difficult to get coverage this time of year. Can you do a Top 10 list of the year based on your expertise? Did you predict a trend in January that happened throughout the year? That can help position you as an industry expert to be used in interviews.

CASE STUDY – I started pitching my product segment ideas to *Good Morning Washington* starting in April. Finally, in August they agreed to have me on. My guess was because it was a slow news time. Then it was up to me to be prepared and give them a great segment, so I was invited back.

TIP #65 – TIMELY TRENDS

Think about things that happen throughout the year to which you might be able to tie a story:

- ❖ Super Bowl Sunday
- ❖ Valentine's Day
- ❖ The Academy Awards
- ❖ St. Patrick's Day
- ❖ Tax Day
- ❖ Mother's or Father's Day
- ❖ Independence Day
- ❖ Halloween
- ❖ The World Series
- ❖ Thanksgiving

It's important to be creative and think outside of the box.

CASE STUDY - One of my favorite stories comes from a Realtor® client, Lizzy, who pitched a Halloween-themed real estate story. It was whether you had to disclose if a house is haunted or a murder took place in it when you sell the home. The story aired on her local CBS news on Halloween. Watch it here: www.PRforAnyone.com/CBSHauntedHouse

TIP #66 – WHAT'S OLD IS NEW AGAIN

The past cannot be changed; the future is still in your power.
~ Hugh White

Do you have an old box of magazines in your attic or basement? Maybe even some of last year's editions in a magazine rack or on your coffee table? Get some inspiration from stories that have already been written. Just tweak an idea or article title and make it current. If someone wrote about it then, why not refresh it and submit the new and improved version?

I see this all the time on television as well. The *Today Show* ran a segment with a nutrition expert on healthy eating at the mall while holiday shopping. When I tried to find the segment for a presentation I was holding, I found a very similar story that ran years earlier on the *Today Show* which was a generic story about what is the healthiest food to eat at the mall.

TIP #67 – BE A STAR

There is a service called Contact Any Celebrity, www.ContactAnyCelebrity.com. This site is a great resource to find celebrities. Contact Any Celebrity provides contact information for celebrities, pubic figures, agents, managers, publicists, and entertainment companies.

Their database has information for over 100,000 people. This is a paid service, but they offer a free trial service, so if you have a list of celebrities for whom you want to obtain contact information, try the free service. If you think contacting celebrities will be something you need to do on a regular basis, then by all means sign-up.

MY FAVORITE TIP – I have been able to find most celebrities' contact information just by using Google. That is how I was able to get to Diana Ross. Remember, Google is a question search engine so ask away.

TIP #68 – DON'T PITCH A PITCH

You hear the word "pitch" all the time, but what I found interesting when interviewing people in the industry is many of them don't want to be "pitched." Instead, why not be different? "Share" your story idea with an editor or reporter versus "pitching them your pitch."

TIP #69 – BEST OF THE BEST

Here is a listing of the Top 20 Most-Read Magazines[1]. If you want to get the most *bang for your buck*—which, in this case, is *free*—try submitting to a magazine with a bigger circulation first.

It will be harder to break into these magazines, but why not try? My motto is, "Go Big or Go Home."

1.	AARP The Magazine	38,600,000
2	People	35,900,000
3	Better Homes & Gardens.	32,500,000
4.	National Geographic Magazine	30,400,000

---
1 Source: Folio

5.	Costco Connection	26,300,000
6.	Good Housekeeping	18,400,000
7.	Reader's Digest	16,900,000
8.	TIME	16,900,000
9.	Sport's Illustrated	16,400,000
10	Southern Living	15,200,000
11	Woman's Day	14,900,000
12	Cosmopolitan	14,200,000
13.	ESPN The Magazine	13,000,000
14,	Taste of Home	12,300,000
15,	Country Living	11,800,000
16.	Family Circle	11,800,000
17.	Food Network Magazine	11,600,000
18.	Men's Health	11,400,000
19.	Women's Health	10,800,000
20.	Game Informer	10,900,000

TIP #70 – DON'T FORGET THE LITTLE GUY

Of course you want to get coverage in a national publication because we all want mass-exposure, but that doesn't mean to only try there. Your success rate will be much higher in local and trade publications. Definitely submit your ideas to them as well. If you are covered in a trade or local publication, use that as a stepping-stone to show a national publication a trend. Pull together similar articles about your type of business and use those to support showing a trend in your industry. Submit a story idea with regards to that and how you can speak to the trend.

TIP #71 – FLY AWAY WITH ME

One of the most captive audiences can be found on an airplane. Doesn't everyone at least flip through the in-air magazine from the seat back pocket at some point during their flight? Over 4.3 billion people flew on airlines servicing the U.S. in 2018. That's a lot of eyes.

Submitting to an in-flight magazine is a very similar process to submitting to a regular publication. However, it is important to note that these types of magazines are looking for compelling long reads. Often their articles are several pages long. A tips list or "best of" idea will likely not be accepted for an in-flight magazine. You also might be better served reaching out to a freelance writer who has written for one of these publications before and submitting your story idea to them.

Also, note that many of the in-flight magazines have an 8-month lead-time so it's important to plan far in advance if you are interested in submitting a story idea to an in-flight magazine. The bonus for this platform – they often pay for stories.

Here are some of the top ranked in-flight magazines in the world:

1) En Route (Air Canada), Enroute.AirCanada.com

2) Open Skies (Emirates, United Arab Emirates), www.OpenSkiesMagazine.com

3) Sky (Delta, US), DeltaSkyMag.delta.com

4) Indwe (SA Express, South Africa), www.FreeMagazines.co.za/index.php/our-magazines/indwe

5) Voyager (British Midland International, United Kingdom), www.VoyagerMagazine.com.au/current-issue/voyager-magazine

6) Smile (Cebu Pacifica, Philippines), www.CebuSmile.com

7) Qantas (Australia), https://www.Qantas.com/travel/airlines/spirit-of-australia/global/en

8) Holland Herald (KLM, Netherlands), Holland-Herald.com

9) Lufthansa Magazine (Germany), https://Magazin.Lufthansa.com/xx/en/

These are some top ranked Airline In-flight Magazines in the U.S.:

1) Sky, DeltaSkyMag.delta.com

2) Hemispheres, www.HemispheresMagazine.com

3) Southwest Airlines Spirit, https://www.SWAMedia.com/magazine

4) American Way, https://Magazines.AA.com

5) Hana Hou!, www.HanaHou.com

6) American Way Celebrated Living, https://American-Way.com/en/celebrated-living

7) American Way Nexos, https://AmericanWay.com/es/nexos

MY FAVORITE TIP – If you have a story idea that is associated with one of an airline's hub cities, try that angle when submitting your idea.

TIP #72 – PLAN AHEAD

Plans are nothing; planning is everything.
~ Dwight D. Eisenhower

Stories for national magazines are usually planned at least four months in advance. Plan your submissions accordingly. If you have a great Back-to-School story idea, you need to submit that story idea in April or early May.

Regional magazines are planned out about two months ahead.

Newspapers and local television are laid out about two weeks ahead (not including breaking news stories), so they have more flexibility versus a national magazine.

TIP #73 – HO HO HOLIDAYS

It's one of the most coveted spots in a magazine, The Annual Holiday Gift Guide. It's so hard to think about Christmas or Hanukkah in the Spring, but if you are trying to have a product featured in a Holiday Gift Guide, you'll need to send in your information as early as May or June. Most Gift Guides for major publications are already closed by early July.

There will be opportunities later in the year for regional publications and newspapers, but for any of the top magazines listed above, send in your ideas no later than the end of June for the best opportunity to be selected for the Gift Guide.

TIP #74 – MARK YOUR CALENDAR

Every magazine has an "editorial calendar" that lists the stories and topics they are going to be writing about and featuring in future editions for the year. It's really geared towards advertisers, but it's a secret tool you can use to find out what's going to be covered in the magazine each month, so you can plan your story ideas accordingly.

As I mentioned above, national magazines have closing dates for content that usually run about four months prior to the issue date, so again, plan your story ideas in advance. Don't send something for the March issue in January. You'll never get in and it's a waste of everyone's time.

Know the editorial calendars and plan your stories around them for the most success. Google the magazine name and either "editorial calendar" or "media kit" to find their annual calendar. Using this resource will help ensure the ideas you are submitting are laser focused to that publication and match exactly what they are looking for and when they need it.

MY FAVORITE TIP – Go through all of the magazines' editorial calendars in which you are interested in and create your own calendar. Mark when and to whom you will need to submit your idea for the best chance of getting covered.

TIP #75 – BE TIMELY

Is there something going on in the news for which you can provide expert opinion? This is your chance. If a reporter has written a story or article and you can add to their information, reach out to them. The same holds true for television. If you see a segment and you have additional information, reach out to that reporter or producer.

They may do a follow-up and include you. Even if that is not the case, but they do respond, you have now gained a media contact. Start cultivating that relationship.

TIP #76 – TO WHOM DO YOU SEND IT?

Are you an expert in your field? Can you provide relevant content on various topics? The media always need resources to whom they can turn. Why not become the expert in your field?

It is critical to know who the right contact person is at every media outlet pertaining to your subject matter. If your expertise is finance, don't send your story to the beauty editor. Find the person who writes articles or is the editor of a section related to your expertise. This person is the one with whom you want to start building a relationship.

Finding the right person will take a little bit of research, but thanks to Google you should be able to find the information quickly.

Another trick is to visit your local library or bookstore and look at the mastheads of newspapers and magazines to find out who the contact person is for your area of expertise.

For newspapers, find out who is generally writing about your topic. Can you provide an alternative angle? Can you create controversy over something they've written about?

Connect with that reporter on social media and comment on articles they've already written. Be sure to mention what you might know about the subject. Start building a rapport with the reporter and developing a relationship. You might just be the next person they turn to when writing on that topic.

💡 TIP #77 – IT'S THAT EASY

So now you know who to contact. How do you find them?

Many of the more mainstream magazines are part of a larger umbrella publishing company such as, Conde Nast, Hearst, Meredith, or Time.

Most large organizations have a common email thread. If you can find one person in the organization (this research is very easy with Google), you will likely be able to figure out your desired contact's email address. Some email thread examples are:

- Conde Nast Publications: firstname_lastname@condenast.com
- Heart Publications: firstnamelastname@hearst.com
- Meredith Publications: firstname.lastname@meredith.com
- Time Publications: firstname_lastname@timeinc.com (acquired by Meredith, 2018)

If you want to reach the editorial office of any of these, call the main switchboard at:

- Conde Nast, 212-286-2860
- Hearst, 212-649-2000
- Meredith (acquired Time in 2018), 212-522-1212

At PR for Anyone® we offer a product with just over 2,300 email strings of television programs, magazines, and newspapers in both the U.S. and Canada. This list can be found at www.PRforAnyone.com/shop.

A great online resource to find publication information is www.MediaBistro.com/mastheads. Type in the publication on which you are looking for information and scroll down to see their contact information including various editors' names, mailing address, and email thread. A quick phone call to the number provided can verify if the person listed is still with the magazine.

Are the editors on social media? Connect with them. Follow them on Twitter and Instagram. Engage with them. Comment about articles they've written. Get to "know" them and *then* send them your idea. In today's electronic world, it really is easy to find and connect with people in the media.

TIP #78 – ANYONE, ANYWHERE

Mondotimes at www.Mondotimes.com is one of my favorite resources for media contact information. This site can link you to the website of any television station, newspaper, magazine, or news radio station in the world. It's also broken down by international, national and local so it's very easy to find exactly what you are looking for. When all else fails, use the phone number on the website and call to ask who is the right contact person.

TIP #79 – GO WITH WHAT YOU KNOW

A trade publication is one of the best forms of PR because that is your target market with a fully engaged audience specifically interested in your topic.

For a listing of trade publications by industry, visit www.Webwire.com/IndustryList.asp.

One of my first media placements was in a trade magazine called *Lower Extremity Review*. I submitted my product for review in their New Product section, and they published it both in print and online. It was the perfect placement for CastMedic Designs because medical professionals who specialize on the lower leg, read the magazine, https://lermagazine.com/products/walking-boot-accessories.

MY FAVORITE TIP – Not sure whom to approach? Find out where your competitors have gotten media coverage and start there.

TIP #80 – SEND A SPECIAL PACKAGE

If there is a media outlet that you really want to break into, consider packaging your idea and sending it in. A friend of mine, Romy Taormina, is the co-founder of Psi-Bands, www.PsiBands.com, a company that manufactures fashionable nausea relief bracelets.

Psi-Bands landed a feature in *Oprah's O Magazine* when they sent one of their editors a package in the mail that delighted and offered the element of surprise. It was delivered in a white gift box with a gift tag on it that said, "Wrap up your nausea." No one could resist opening that up. Inside the gift box they included a few sets of Psi Bands and their brochure. The magazine feature was entitled *Grace Under Pressure* and was included on *Oprah's List* of favorite things.

MY FAVORITE TIP – Be very strategic when you do this. Ideally, let the editor or producer know to expect a package. When Slawsa was on the *Today Show*, it was because Dylan Dryer said on a previous show how she loved to top her hotdogs. The founder of Slawsa sent her a case of the gourmet topping and wrote a note letting her know she had seen the segment. Slawsa was then featured on the *Today Show* for National Hotdog Day.

TIP #81 – A SIDE JOB

Do you have a story to tell? Many magazines accept articles from freelancers and even pay for them. From writing about your topic for a business publication to the story behind your business, if it's compelling for a publication, there are places you can have an article published. Visit www.PRforAnyone.com/Freelancing for resources on freelancing.

Many publications also have guidelines for freelance articles on their website.

CASE STUDY – I submitted an article entitled *5 Tips for DIY PR* to *American Business Magazine* that was published. Freelancing is a great way to share your knowledge or your story in a way that is not self-promotion. Of course I received a by-line in the article, so my bio and website were included.

TIP #82 – STOP THE PRESSES!

A great website that lists every newspaper in the country is www.USNPL.com.

From this site, you are able to link to any newspaper and find contact information.

It is important to remember though, as much as we would all love to start out with a big feature in the *Wall Street Journal*, that probably isn't going to happen.

The easiest newspaper to land exposure with is your local paper. Most community papers will cover a new business, especially if you can come up with a unique hook.

Find the reporter or reporters who cover your topic and approach them directly.

From there, continue trying with regional and then national papers in your area.

Your Name in Lights

*Enthusiasm is the yeast that makes your hopes shine to the stars.
Enthusiasm is the sparkle in your eyes,
the swing in your gait, the grip of your hand,
the irresistible surge of will and energy to execute your ideas.
~ Henry Ford*

You might be reading this book thinking to yourself, "Maybe she just got lucky. The average person isn't going to appear on national television. It's not realistic."

You've seen so far in this book how I landed a regular appearance on television, how Jennifer Fugo appeared on *Dr. Oz* twice in thirty days, how Patricia was used as an industry expert on her CBS Morning show, how Slawsa ended up on the *Today Show* and many more. In this chapter, you are going to learn about several other people, just like you and me, who have successfully pitched television segments – locally and nationally. The one thing they all have in common is that they used the *Get PR Famous Formula* and followed the system.

PR success is built through relationships and perseverance. If one thing doesn't work, try again with something else. By consistently submitting good, quality, newsworthy story ideas, you will end up in the media.

TIP #83 – START AT HOME

A goal properly set, is halfway reached.
~ Zig Ziglar

Landing a spot on national television is often referred to as the "crown jewel" of media coverage. It is important to understand, however, that it is highly (and I emphasize *highly*) unlikely that you will be asked to appear on national television as an expert without some local television experience under your belt. This notion holds true especially on a live program. The producers have to be certain you will make a good guest. They can't risk having someone on-air who might freeze or who does not speak clearly and knowledgeably about their topic.

Local television is your stepping-stone to national television. Barring the top local television markets that can be a little harder to crack, it should be relatively easy to get a local television appearance if you have something newsworthy to share.

I am not saying you can't get on-air in a top market; just be prepared for it to be more difficult and take more time. It took me five months to get on ABC in Washington, D.C. (#6 market – see below). If you happen to live or work in a smaller market share area, you will probably be able to land a spot on the air sooner than if you are in a larger market share area. The reasoning behind this logic is that the larger market share stations are receiving more story submissions than the smaller stations because they have a larger audience and can expose people to more potential customers.

If you are trying to get on a smaller market station that is not local to you, tie your story into something local in that area. Perhaps you went to school there, worked for a locally based company, or can specifically help people in that area? A local station is going to want a local angle. Get creative and discover what makes you newsworthy to them and their audience.

The Top 10 Local Television Markets are:

1. New York
2. Los Angeles
3. Chicago
4. Philadelphia
5. Dallas-Ft. Worth
6. Washington, D.C.
7. Houston
8. San Francisco-Oakland-San Jose
9. Boston
10. Atlanta

EXPERT TIP – At my very first job producing television at *The Oprah Winfrey Show*, I learned how to be uncompromising in my search for the most niche expert at the top of their industry with the most current and relevant information to add. Be that person. Have something unique to say. Personality is a must, must, must—you must engage me. If I don't want to listen to you, I can't expect millions of viewers to want to, right? I must respect and like you the minute I lay eyes on you or it's over. So many experts today don't know how to present themselves—their walking brand—properly. My advice is threefold—know your brand inside out, know yourself and how you are being received, and understand how the television industry works—what producers are looking for and how to fill that need—how you fit into the solution. ~ Natalie Mashaal, former Producer, *The Oprah Winfrey Show*

TIP #84 – WHO, WHAT, WHEN, WHERE?

The first person to contact at a local news station is the assignment editor. They are the idea people with their fingers on the pulse of the community, and they are the ones who submit ideas up the ladder to production.

Due to the high number of submissions television stations receive, your idea will need to stand out in that sea of email. The first thing they see is the subject line of your email. Make it catchy so they want to read more. Next, make sure your email is short and easy to read. A wordy email will likely be deleted. They just don't have the time to read lengthy emails.

When submitting an idea, know where it fits into their programming. Many news programs do not have guests in their main news slots at 5:00 pm, 6:00 pm, and 11:00 pm, but check what they offer in terms of morning and/or mid-day shows and submit your ideas specifically for those programs.

Local news stations read local blogs, community papers and scour social media to get ideas for their show. So, if you are covered in any of these publications, use those stories when you send your idea to the local station. Local television stations really do want to feature local businesses and guests; but remember to be creative with your ideas so it's something easy for them to work with and appealing to their viewers.

TIP #85 – THINK BIG, START SMALL

Did you know that many local stories are filmed and edited in a way so they can be shared with affiliates across the country? A story that is evergreen and has a general topic is filmed so that any anchor can fill in and give their opening report and then they roll the story.

CASE STUDY - I mentioned my client Matt and his book, *The A.D.D. Entrepreneur* earlier. We landed him a segment on his local NBC by pitching a medical/business angle highlighting how someone with A.D.D. can have a very successful business. The story was shared through NBC's affiliate network and aired across the country with different anchors providing their introduction leading into Matt's story. This extended coverage exposed Matt and his book to millions of viewers.

Here is the segment so you can envision how any on-air host could run this story and make it their own, www.PRforAnyone.com/ADDEntrepreneur.

TIP #86 – GO FOR IT

When I saw a picture of Savannah Guthrie, Host of the *Today Show* in a medical boot, I was sure I was going to land a spot on the *Today Show*. I had been doing this type of pitching for years now and I knew exactly what to do and how to do it. What I didn't realize when I pitched my story idea is that it was Sweeps Month (February). This is when television programs are rated, and the highest rated shows get to charge the most for advertising. The shows save their biggest celebrities for this time in the ratings race. Regrettably, the *Today Show* was not going to feature Christina Daves of Gainesville, Virginia.

I was determined not to miss out on this opportunity. I had a poster made and superimposed my product on Savannah's boot. I bought a bus ticket and made my way to the NBC Plaza in New York City.

Hey Savannah You can HEAL IN STYLE!

www.HealInStyle.com

When I arrived bright and early on that brisk February morning, the NBC Plaza was filling up; but over by the glass where you can see into where the anchors are, there was no one. I couldn't believe it. I ran over to the glass and peered in and there were only two people there, Savannah and the person putting on her microphone. I put my poster up to the glass and the studio tech gave me the thumbs up. Mouthing through the plate glass I said, "Show Savannah." She turned around and mouthed back, "Oh my gosh! I love it!" I replied with, "I have a goodie bag for you when you come out." I did my homework and I knew that the anchors come out to the Plaza for a short segment.

This was it! I knew it was going to happen. I headed over to my spot on the rail with my poster and my decorated boot in hand and waited. But then it happened, the worst possible news I could get.

The person who runs the Plaza told me they couldn't show me, or my boot, or my poster on air. They aren't permitted to "promote" products because they have advertisers. When I told him that Savannah was coming to see me, he said, "If she does and you're on air, you can't say your company or product name." I felt as if I'd been punched in the stomach. I came all this way and was so close. I was ready to cry.

A few minutes later the universe opened. To this day, I don't know what happened, but the Plaza Manager ran over to me and said, "You're going to be featured in every intro and outro – get excited!" Savannah was in the studio talking about "The Boot Lady" so the camera panned on me repeatedly. Sirius XM's Today Show Radio came over and interviewed me. And Savannah came out and said, "We just gave you a ton of airtime, I hope it does a lot for your business." She was lovely and I realized then, if you work hard, are kind, and give to others, sometimes really good things can happen to you too.

CastMedic Designs is featured on the Today Show after Savannah Guthrie is in a medical boot

TIP #87 – YOUR "SIZZLE"

We are all of us stars, and we deserve to twinkle.
~ Marilyn Monroe

Once you've garnered a few local media appearances, it's important to put those together into a media reel, also known as a "sizzle reel." This video is a short montage of you on television discussing your expertise. A reel can easily be created with programs such as iMovie on your computer. There are also companies who specialize in creating these reels. You can also look for freelancers on Craig's List. Or, if you have a university close by with a film school, see if you can get a student to help you. You want this to be high quality as this is your first impression with a television assignment editor or producer.

TIP #88 – MAKE IT EASY FOR THEM

If you don't tell your story, someone else will.
~ Unknown

Make it easy for a producer by providing a full layout of how you envision the segment will go. Refer back to TIP #30, where we show you an easy email layout to use when submitting your segment idea. Come up with a catchy hook that they can use to introduce the segment. If you are submitting to a national television station, include your sizzle reel as well. As always, keep it simple and easy to read. Make it easy for the producer to visualize the segment.

TIP #89 – BE OUR GUEST

Many of the syndicated talk shows have a "Be on the Show" section on their website. Listed here will be topics they are covering or guests needed for future segments. If you fit into a category for which they are requesting guests, submit using the online form. These are frequently updated so check back often.

Every season there are new talk shows popping up. Set a Google Alert to keep you posted on new shows. You will have a better chance appearing on a new show that is trying to fill their shows than a top-rated established show. Once you know about the new shows, don't forget to check their "Be a Guest" section.

MY FAVORITE TIP – The television production industry is actually quite small. Most of the associate and senior producers all know one another. When a talk show is canceled, many of those producers move to one of the new shows that are replacing the canceled show. This is why building relationships is such an important component of PR.

TIP #90 – CHECK THE CLASSIFIEDS

Talk shows filmed in New York, Chicago, and Los Angeles often post guest queries on Craig's List. National shows have travel budgets, so they often try to find guests in their production cities to cut down on those costs. Don't let geography stop you from reaching out to them. I am located in Washington, D.C. so the trip to New York is relatively short. For a national appearance on a show taping in New York, it is worth it for me to pay my own travel expenses. If the opportunity arises to appear on a national show and you are not local to them, offer to pay the travel expenses for your first appearance.

TIP #91 – HARO-ING FOR TV

Starting in August, until around April, many nationally syndicated shows put out guest requests on HARO. Most of these shows are on hiatus over the summer and don't film. But come August, they are frequently searching for guests on various topics, and the producers are in a hurry to fill segments. This time of year is a great time to monitor HARO closely to see if there is a fit.

TIP #92 – SOCIAL "NETWORKING"

Make connections with television shows you are interested in appearing on through social media. They often post guest requests on both Facebook and Twitter. Stay active in discussions on these sites as well, as you might catch the eye of a producer working on a particular segment.

For Twitter, I recommend finding particular producers and reporters, following them, and interacting directly. The hosts themselves don't do any booking. Keep in mind, you probably aren't going to have much luck interacting with someone like Ellen DeGeneres who is nearing 100 million Twitter followers.

CASE STUDY – My client, Susan, is a home stager. She was on Twitter and saw a reporter from her local NBC station looking for a real estate agent to talk about Amazon's HQ2 coming to her area. Susan jumped on the story and said she had staged a home in that area and she could be there at 4:00 pm when he needed an expert for that segment. Although he was looking for an agent, he used a stager because she could meet his time demands and he tweaked the story accordingly. Watch Susan's segment here: www.PRforAnyone.com/Susan.

TIP #93 – WHERE DO I FIND YOU?

*And, when you want something,
all the universe conspires in helping you to achieve it.*
~ Paulo Coelho, The Alchemist

If appearing on television is your dream, watch the program you would like to be on and become aware of their format so your story ideas are on-target. You can often find individual producer information at the end of the show in the credits. Another way to find out this information is to simply Google the segment name and topic and look for the name of the producer via your search. Keep in mind that television talk shows have multiple producers, so if one does not respond, try another.

Many television producers are on LinkedIn. Connect with them by providing value. Don't submit a pitch on your initial connection request. Once they connect, follow up with a note referencing them or something in their profile. Offer to provide assistance on a future story and invite them to review your profile for more information.

Remember, producers are looking for you. They have the daunting task of coming up with new material daily. You have information they want and need. Most producers I have reached out to have accepted my LinkedIn invitation to connect. I then become another potential resource for them.

One important thing to learn about is the hierarchy of television. Although the producer is the top of the totem pole, your best bet is to actually build a relationship with an intern or production assistant. They are on the pulse of what's hot and trending, and they submit their ideas to the producer. They are also tasked by the producer to find good guests and experts.

Interns and production assistants are the ones with whom you want to connect. They are working toward becoming a producer someday, so you are continuing to build good future relationships.

They are usually younger people and very active on social media. Find them on Twitter and/or Instagram and, if they have a Facebook page affiliated with their television show, connect there. Do not try to connect with them personally on Facebook unless you have built a relationship with them and have become friends.

For local television, pick up the phone and call the station. Ask them which producer covers your topic. Business…Fashion…Health…and ask for their email address. It's really that easy!

MY FAVORITE TIP – I can assure you that there has never been a newsroom who answered the phone and said, "I'm sorry! We're not taking any new stories today." It will never happen so don't be afraid to pick up the phone and call.

<u>CASE STUDY</u> – I had connected with a producer from the Dr. Oz show on LinkedIn. When she realized how connected I was on that platform she would often ask me if I knew of guests for stories on which she was working. One day she asked if I knew anyone who had parents with dementia. My friend and colleague Kay owns a company, Memory Banc, www.MemoryBanc.com, that assists with finances for family members with memory loss. We were able to secure her a place on the show, which was tremendous for her business.

Kay Bransford, MemoryBanc, on Dr. Oz discussing dementia

💡 TIP #94 – WHERE DO YOU FIT IN THE PUZZLE?

What I have learned about landing media is that every outlet has a puzzle that they are making pieces fit into. I mentioned earlier about doing your homework. Knowing the types of stories a media outlet covers will put you ahead of your competition. How do you fit into their format? If you can make it easy for the producer to visualize how you would be on a segment and appeal to their audience, it will be easier to get the "yes."

When I started pitching my idea of a regular product segment to my local morning shows, I made sure I pitched the stations that had this type of programming. If I had pitched this to my local NBC station, they would have scratched their heads because they do not air a morning show in this format. Instead, I did my homework and pitched my local ABC station and eventually landed a regular spot on *Good Morning Washington*.

CASE STUDY - My client Jodi, an inventor, from Tulsa was trying to get media coverage for her product; instead of pitching just the product by itself, she knew that her local CBS station covers "Hometown Hero" stories. Jodi uses college students who are paying their own tuition and women who have left abusive relationships to assemble her product. Watch her segment at www.PRforAnyone.com/ZippedMe.

Zipped Me is featured in a Hometown Hero story on CBS in Tulsa

TIP #95 – NO STALKING PLEASE

I have heard repeatedly in my interviews with television producers that follow-up communication is okay. Please don't hound them though, and don't continue to submit the same idea over and over, trying to convince them how great the idea is. You never want to imply to a producer that they are not doing their job.

Producers are very busy and most shows are on tight budgets, so these producers are over-worked as it is. Try an email follow up. If it's a time-sensitive idea on a current hot story, give them a call. If they don't respond, wait a month or so and submit another story idea.

MY FAVORITE TIP — Do not contact producers while they are on the air or during taping. Obviously, you know when live shows are on-air. For other shows, call the main number and ask when they tape. Show them you respect their position and email or call producers during their off-air time.

TIP #96 – PAY TO "PLAY"

Pay-to-play is also known as entertainment branding. Basically, you pay someone who has the contacts in the industry to guarantee placement on a television show. Very rarely would this exposure be on the *Today Show* or *Good Morning America* and if so, it would be extremely expensive. Think of it more as advertising, since you are paying to have you or your business/product featured on a television show.

It is extremely important to look at the return on investment (ROI) if you decide to go this route. If, for example, you sell ski apparel and your contact has placement capability in Florida, is that really a good idea? Research the markets and the company doing the placing. Make sure it is a good fit and the investment is worth the exposure you will get out of the appearance.

TIP #97 – IT'S ALL ABOUT YOU

> *Eighty percent of success is showing up.*
> ~ Woody Allen

You've done all the work I mentioned here and it finally happens, you get a television appearance! Now what? The scariest part about your first television appearance is not knowing what to expect. It's the fear of the unknown. I want to take some of the mystery out of it for you, so you can relax and enjoy it, because it really is a lot of fun.

Many segments are aired live but the producer should let you know whether you will be live or taped. Even if it's taped, the show often does not want to edit it, so I recommend you act as if it's live.

If the show does not provide transportation to the studio, they will tell you what time to arrive. Make sure you are on time. You can't keep live television waiting.

When you arrive, the production assistant or associate producer will take you to the "green room" (waiting room or lounge) before going on-air. If it's a national show, the room usually has yummy treats. (Of course, on your first appearance, you'll probably be too nervous to eat anything.) Most national programs provide hair and makeup, so you wait in the green room until the associate producer comes to get you. If it's a local show, you should be ready to go on-air when your producer or host arrives.

Turn your cell phone off. I was surprised how small the actual television studios are, and it is important to watch your noise level as they are likely filming something else while you are preparing for your segment.

A sound tech will come in to put a microphone on you. There is a small transmitter that attaches to your backside, and a wire they will run from the transmitter, under your clothes, and clip to your lapel. A very important note, when you are mic'ed, the sound people on the other end can hear everything you are saying and doing. Make sure you use the restroom before they put your microphone on, and be careful of what you say because someone is listening on the other end.

Most television appearances are conversational, so don't worry about talking into a specific camera. The host will likely use the teleprompter and introduce you. It's okay to look at the camera/ teleprompter then too, but then adjust to your host. You can always ask them before you air where they want you to look.

Usually the host will be prepared with questions and guide the interview, but you should always be prepared for the host who isn't ready for the segment. Be ready to talk about your topic for three to four minutes, which is the average time for a television segment.

This scenario happened to me in one of my first television interviews. I had to literally take over the interview, and luckily it ended up fine, but always be prepared for things not going as anticipated.

Prepare yourself ahead of time for the host who is passive, the host who is antagonistic (how can you re-direct or guide it to be more positive?), or the host who asks non-relevant questions. (We'll address these situations later in this section.)

Some tips while on camera:

- Be warm, approachable and sincere.
- Know your topic.
- If standing, don't lock your knees, relax.
- If possible, keep your feet on the floor so you don't swing your feet.
- Keep your hands in your lap or rest them on the arm of the chair.
- Be comfortable.
- Don't cross your arms.
- Always Smile. Even with a serious topic, a sympathetic, thoughtful smile gives you a human connection.
- Make sure that you remain smiling until you know for certain your segment is over.
- Most of the daytime variety shows are looking for guests with lots of passion and energy.
- Don't get up until the producer tells you to do so.

The host should mention the name of your company at some point during the interview. If the host does not, and you can find a way to interject it, doing it once is okay. Remember your job is to serve their audience, not yourself, so repeatedly saying your company name is a good way to *not* get invited back.

It is not appropriate to give your website address on-air unless specifically asked. You should also check if they will be running your information on a news ticker during your interview. If so, make sure you provide the show with this information to ensure accuracy.

Lastly, be a courteous guest that they will want to invite back. If you act as if you are a prima donna and should be treated as such, I can almost guarantee they won't want to have you back. I always leave my television appearances with big hugs and "thank yous" to everyone, which is much more appreciated than having an entitled attitude.

EXPERT TIP – What is the biggest blunder a guest can make? Making it all about them, rather than meeting the needs of the audience. The interviewee keeps saying their company name, their book, their product, their website. It annoys the heck out of a reporter. And, rambling with no solid sound bites. People get nervous and don't speak coherently. Three sentences, then they're done. Relationship is the name of the game, hence the interview is a conversation, not a one-sided monologue. ~ Shawne Duperon, Media Coach & Trainer, 6-Time EMMY® Award Winner, www.ShawneTV.com.

TIP #98 – POLISH YOUR PITCH WITH THE PRO

My producer on *Good Morning Washington* is Kyle Ridley. He posted this on his Instagram account (@ProducerKyle) and gave me permission to use it in this book. It really gives you an incredible perspective of what a television producer is looking for in a pitch and in a guest.

Follow his recommendations. He is the one on the other end receiving pitches and he is the one who will give you the "yes." Having interviewed and spoken with many television producers, Kyle is speaking for all television producers out there. This is what they are all looking for in guests:

A strong guest knows the essentials of a strong pitch:

- ❖ Keep it short and compelling. Producers get hundreds of pitches a day and rarely have time to read a lengthy email.

- ❖ Call if you'd like, but you're likely going to be directed to email the details. It's rare to get a "yes" right away on a phone pitch. Again, bookers are inundated with calls and it's often easier to visually sort through them in an inbox.

- ❖ Make sure to include past media appearances if you have them. If the topic sounds interesting, the first thing I'm going to ask for is past media or some sort of clip to get a feel of your on-air presence.

- ❖ Do not worry if you've never been on air, but be prepared to jump on a call and also offer background material (website, social media, IG videos)

- ❖ Think about the viewer. What will their takeaway be? Pitching a profile just about you isn't going to resonate with a booker – whose main focus is the viewer. What will they want to take action on after your segment?

- ❖ We're looking for personality, energy, emotion and visuals.

- ❖ Bringing energy doesn't mean you have to be bouncing off the walls, but we want to keep audiences engaged and awake (especially morning TV).

- ❖ Bringing emotion doesn't mean we need tears, but what is it that will tug at heartstrings?

- ❖ Be succinct. Most segments are 3-5 minutes long.

- ❖ If you are doing any sort of demo, make sure you're prepared to bring a mighty display. I always send strong examples of past segments to let people know what we expect. TV is visual and if you want to do a cooking or DIY segment – you should be prepared to cover a large table with multiple dishes, drinks and décor.

- ❖ If you're doing a sit-down interview – be prepared to have photos and/or video that can be used to supplement the discussion. If you don't have those, make sure to offer suggested graphics that can be made.

- ❖ Be ready to be invited back and keep the ideas coming! If you knock it out of the park, a producer is likely going to add you to their roster of regulars.

TIP #99 – LEARNING TO TALK

A sound bite is a succinct way to get your message across. An average sound bite is about five to eight seconds and covers what you want to say about one specific point. Speaking in soundbites is important for both television and radio because it prevents rambling and incoherency in the interview.

Watch the interview I did with Charlotte Graham, veteran television producer and founder of 360º Speaking about soundbites www.PRforAnyone.com/Soundbites. In her response on speaking in sound bites, she unintentionally answered in soundbites. It's a great way to learn how to use them.

TIP #100 – YA'LL COME BACK NOW

*If a man be gracious and courteous to strangers,
it shows he is a citizen of the world.*
~ Francis Bacon

So now you've made it. You've been a guest. How do you keep getting asked back? Of course, most importantly is to be a good guest. Authenticity is vital to be asked to return. You have to be able to relate to the audience. Have energy. Get your message out and be excited about it. Be comfortable on camera so you don't come across as unauthentic or unbelievable.

"Be nice to everyone" is my motto at home with my kids. I have instilled that value in them since the early days of playgroups. Be nice to the page who walks you down the hall. Be nice to the makeup artist who makes you look fabulous on-air (if applicable). Be nice to the assistant producer who gets you ready for your interview. How you treat people at the show goes a long way in determining whether or not they want you back.

Lastly, be accessible and available to them when they need you. Respond immediately to emails and if they need you in-studio tomorrow, drop everything and say, "Of course!" Be the type of guest they need, someone who can accommodate their crazy production schedules.

CASE STUDY – When I got a call from my local FOX station saying one of the morning anchors broke her foot and was in a boot and could I be there in-studio at 7:00 am tomorrow to decorate it on air? I immediately said, "Yes!" Check out that segment at www.PRforAnyone.com/GoodDayDC.

Christina on Good Day DC Dressing-up an Anchor's Boot

TIP #101 – WORST-CASE SCENARIO

*When we face the worst that can happen
in any situation, we grow.
~ Elisabeth Kubler Ross*

When doing a television interview, it is vital that you are fully prepared for anything. Would you know what to do if your host wasn't prepared for your segment? You have to be able to confidently take control of the interview and make sure you can bring it back to the topic. What if a host is speaking on and on and you can barely get a word in? Are you self-assured enough to find a break in the conversation and share your message? What if the host says your name or your company name wrong? How do you rectify this situation? Maybe they are just having a bad day and it takes its toll on your interview. Would you be able to handle any of these situations?

If you plan to be a regular expert on local television, and eventually national television, I recommend media training. Professionals will put you in these situations doing mock interviews and guide you through the appropriate responses. They can also help you put your message into succinct sound bites for various interviews whether it is the standard three to four-minute interview or perhaps a longer one.

I recommend working with a media trainer who has significant television experience and can prepare you for any scenario. In the event you are placed in any of these situations and you rebound successfully, it adds to your credibility as a strong guest.

TIP #102 – LOOKING GOOD

I learned about the need for television makeup the hard way. I had no idea that most local television stations don't have hair and makeup artists on staff. A local show in a top television market such as New York or Chicago might have a makeup artist, but even in Washington, D.C., the #6 market in the country, the local television stations don't provide this service.

Early on, I was on a local program in Texas and wore a white shirt and had on light makeup. I looked like a ghost! I wish someone had told me about the bright lights used in television studios and the need for heavier makeup than my everyday wear. Feel free to see what *not* to do with makeup when you land a television appearance, www.PRforAnyone.com/KENS5.

The lights used in television studios are very bright and intense, and it is very important to wear the appropriate makeup. My best recommendation is to have your makeup done professionally, if at all possible. Find a local makeup artist or visit a store like M-A-C at your local mall, https://www.maccosmetics.com/stores.

Often, however, local appearances are not scheduled until the very last minute. I got a call at 7:00 p.m. asking if I could be at the local *NBC* station by 9:00 a.m. the next morning. In that case, I had no way to schedule anything.

It is important to know how to apply your own television makeup, just in case. We were very fortunate to have Tracey Garcia, veteran makeup artist at *FOX News*, and a freelance makeup artist in the Washington, D.C. area, www.TraceyGarciaMakeupArtist.com share television makeup tips for women, www.PRforAnyone.com/TVMakeupforWomen.

Men, you also need to think about makeup. The studio lights can make you look green. If you have facial hair, it is important to know how to cover that up a bit. Tracey offers a segment on men's makeup as well. Gentleman, learn what needs to be in your makeup bag, www.PRforAnyone.com/TVMakeupforMen.

TIP #103 – WHAT TO WEAR WHERE

Fashion fades, only style remains the same.
~ Coco Chanel

You've got your TV makeup figured out. Now, what do you wear? The easiest thing to do is watch the show and see what the host and other guests are wearing and dress comparably. If you're on a business show, wear business attire, as you want to be taken seriously.

Make sure you are comfortable in whatever you are wearing. If not, it could affect how you hold yourself on camera. Remember, you want to appear relaxed, comfortable and authentic on television.

Avoid solid white, all black, and busy patterns. Find out if they use a green screen and if so, don't wear green. The same holds true if the news program regularly uses a blue background; don't wear blue.

Bright colors are great for TV. When you go on a national show, they will often ask you to bring several outfits, and then a wardrobe person will pick your outfit based on what the host is wearing and if there are other people in the segment as well.

For women, scarves and dangling jewelry are distracting and should be avoided. Men, don't wear short socks.

TIP #104 – YOU GOT THE AXE

You learn how to be a gracious winner and an outstanding loser.
~ Joe Namath

As heartbreaking as it is, getting bumped from a show happens. Don't take it personally. This scenario is somewhat common on live television, especially if there is breaking news. It can also happen at the last minute when a segment is canceled in favor of something else or a decision is made to run another segment longer.

The most important thing you can do when this situation happens is to remain gracious. Your ultimate goal is to be invited back, and if you come off irritated or angry with the producer, you will likely not be invited back for a future segment.

The television production world is very small, and the last thing you would want is to be blacklisted as a difficult guest. Be thankful, appreciative and remember that you now have a relationship with this producer so you can continue to offer future segment ideas.

I'll share my national television heartache…I was asked to send a decorated medical boot to the 4th hour of the Today Show, and the segment was booked. I watched and waited with nervous anticipation. The hour kept ticking away, and then the show ended, no CastMedic Designs. I had officially been bumped. The good news is I've built a relationship with that producer.

In fact, when I suggested to my alma mater, Virginia Tech, that we should do an event with Hoda Kotb, anchor of the *Today Show*, and former alumnus as well, they said they didn't know how to reach her. I went back to that producer and was able to connect with Hoda, put together an event with her, and I was actually the one who got to interview her, www.PRforAnyone.com/HodaKotbInterview.

Christina interviews Hoda Kotb, co-anchor of the Today Show about her rise to success at NBC

TIP #105 – COPY THAT

Make sure you know of a company who can record any of your television appearances. There are many companies who have access to stations and programming across the country. Often the television station can direct you to someone as well. Use this footage on your website and to gain more media exposure. Most shows will allow you to use your segment on your own social media sites and in future marketing. However, some will not and have strict copyright rules, so make sure you know their policies and only use footage you are permitted to share. Many shows now post video clips directly to their website and, if that is the case, you are permitted to use the footage for your personal distribution. Remember, once you land some media exposure, it will open your opportunities to more and continue to add to your credibility.

TIP #106 – RIDE THE WAVE

*We must learn to apply all that we know
so we can attract all that we want.
~ Jim Rohn*

You've worked and worked and you finally get a PR hit. Now what? Tell the world because media begets media.

After I taped the S*teve Harvey Show,* I had a few weeks before it aired. It aired on our local *NBC* affiliate, so I sent them an email saying a local business would be on the show November 1st and would they want to cover it on the daytime news program before the *Steve Harvey Show* aired that day? It worked and they invited me to appear on the show. I filmed an entire segment all about my products, and they asked for a lot of visuals so I was able to bring every decorated boot I had. That gave me yet another television appearance and more credibility. www.PRforAnyone.com/NBCWRC4.

CastMedic Designs is featured on NBC in Washington, D.C. before the Steve Harvey Show airs

After Diana Ross was photographed wearing a CastMedic Designs' product, I contacted the producer of the *Steve Harvey Show* with whom I had worked. Steve Harvey ended up airing an entire segment on my company and me, to show how successful his Top Inventor was becoming. He said, "If THE Diva, the Diva of Diva's, Diana Ross is wearing it, you know it has to be good!" And he showed the press photo of her wearing the product. This kind of exposure is priceless. www.PRforAnyone.com/SteveHarveyUpdate.

Remember to think outside of the box when you land media exposure. Consider who would be interested in knowing you appeared on a certain show or in a publication, and what you can spin from it.

TIP #107 – WHAT'S YOUR REALITY?

Reality is merely an illusion, albeit a very persistent one.
~ Albert Einstein

Love it or hate it, reality television is here to stay. There are many PR opportunities in this realm. As I'm sure you know, "reality" television is actually quasi-scripted, so there are numerous possibilities for you or your business to be featured in a reality-themed show.

First and foremost, calculate the risk of reality television. You have no say in how you will be portrayed, so if there is any possibility that you or your product may not be presented in the best light, ask yourself what this depiction could mean for your business. There is the old adage that "any publicity is good publicity," but you'll have to make that decision ahead of time. Look at famous reality television actors such as Snookie or Omarosa. Even with a negative image, they have become very well-known and successful.

On the other hand, reality television can catapult fame. There is Elisabeth Hasselbeck who appeared on *Survivor*. She spent many years as a host of *The View* and an anchor on *Fox & Friends*. Or, Bethenny Frankel, who was on *The Real Housewives of New York City*. She has since sold her Skinnygirl cocktail line for over 100 million dollars and was the host of her own daytime talk show.

If you decide this medium is the route for you, the person to contact is the talent producer or the talent executive for that show. You can find those names in the credits at the end of the program. Just like a magazine or television story idea, prepare the same type of submission for reality television. Put a good creative idea together and submit it. You will probably want to include a video with your submission because of the nature of this type of programming and their need to see your personality on camera.

EXPERT TIP – Pitching yourself, or your show, as an unknown talent can be challenging. On one hand, most production companies will not review unsolicited pitch materials due to previous industry-known legal situations surrounding intellectual property and copyright violations. On the other hand, how do you pitch yourself, or your show, to a creative exec that actually gets their attention? Here are some ways that have worked for me:

Meet creatives and network execs on LinkedIn. The corporate entertainment industry (tv buyers) is unpredictable and always changing. Most of the producers, developers and buyers I know are all on LinkedIn. Write an awesome article that gets traction and then send it to the creative exec. Don't bog them down with what you want to do, show them what you're already doing. If I can help make an intro for you, and it's the right fit, reach out and introduce yourself to me on LinkedIn.com/in/yoitsvinnie.

Producers are listening to podcasts. Network executives are listening to podcasts. We live in an audible age of media. In a make-it-to-take-it economy you need to make your podcast so you can take it to the next level with a broadcast partner. NBC Digital is scooping up podcasts as we speak, incubating them on their digital network while retaining unscripted rights for Oxygen and scripted rights to NBC/Bravo. Many broadcast networks have recently launched competitive podcast networks as well. This will be a great way to get your foot in the door. Prove the audience is there before you pitch your project. Show the demand.

Stay in touch with meaningful updates. If you don't have anything new to add to the convo, then wait. If an exec isn't responding to your messages, then limit your updates to 2-4 times a year. Don't assume they aren't interested: no response is not the same as "no thanks." If anything, assume they aren't quite picking up what you're putting down... yet. Sometimes, being too early or ahead of the game works against you. Build a long-standing relationship with them and when the timing is right, they will know exactly how and where to find you. ~ Vinnie Potestivo, www.VPETalent.com

TIP #108 – PRODUCT PLACEMENT

Do you want to see your product on television? Is there a particular show or character on a show that you could see using your product? If so, reach out to them! Again, it's really that easy.

The first thing to do is call the main network and ask for the number of the show you are trying to reach. Before you call the show directly, you'll need to know if you want the costume designer or the prop master. If it's clothing related (purses, jewelry, shoes, etc.), ask for the costume designer. For anything on set, ask for the prop master.

I keep telling you to pick up the phone because reaching someone in the media really is that easy.

Obviously, I have a very unique product, but I have spoken with the costume designers of all the major medical shows and emailed them information. If there is a storyline with someone in a medical boot, at least they know where to come to make it fashionable.

Here are the main numbers to all of the mainstream media companies:

ABC — 212-456-7777
A&E — 212-210-1400
BET — 202-608-2000
CBS — 818-655-5000//310-575-7000
CW — 818-977-2500
DISNEY CHANNEL — 818-569-7500
E! ENTERTAINMENT — 323-954-2400
FOX — 310-369-1000
HBO — 212-512-1000
LIFETIME — 212-424-7000
NICKELODEON — 212-258-7579
NBC UNIVERSAL — 212-413-5000/818-840-4444

Find out about new shows and television pilots at www.ProductionWeekly.com.

EXPERT TIP – TV and movies tell stories about people and the clothing or decor needs to reflect their persona to get their character across to the audience. Be sure you have watched the TV show and are 100% sure your product "fits" the character you are going after. Once you are confident about it being a good match, calling will be so much easier. ~ Sarah Shaw, www.SarahShawConsulting.com. Her handbags were seen in movies including, *Ocean's 11*, *America's Sweethearts*, and *Legally Blonde* and the television shows *Friends* and *Will and Grace*.

Radio-Active

*TV gives everyone an image, but radio gives birth
to a million images in a million brains*
~ Peggy Noonan

I love giving podcast and radio interviews. It's like chatting with a friend, just hanging out while getting to share what I love with thousands of listeners, and no one knows when I'm having a hair-for-radio day. Radio is easier than TV because the audience cannot judge you based on appearances. I've given radio interviews after working out, in my pajamas, with no makeup on and my hair in a ponytail. That being said, you have to be able to carry an interview based on your voice and inflection and keep the listener engaged.

In TIP #99 we talked about the soundbite. It's even more important to be engaging on radio and allow your voice to provide visuals for the listener. Speak succinctly to get your point across. This technique is just as important with radio as it is with television. Be prepared for a radio interview. Silence is deafening on radio so make sure you're ready to go.

TIP #109 – PODCASTERS' PARADISE

A great place to start is with the podcast. There are over 750,000 podcasts with over 124 million listeners. This is a great medium to become comfortable with being interviewed. I used to be so nervous that I would do podcasts down in my basement with several bottles of water guzzling them down when the host was asking me questions.

People often discount the podcast but where else can you find an audience completely targeted to your expertise? Even if they only have a few thousand downloads per month, that is a few thousand of your ideal customer. When pitching yourself to a podcast, stay focused on the audience and the value you can bring to them. Check out what they have already covered and what topic you can offer that is new and provides value to their listeners.

Christina as a guest on Barry Moltz's Small Business Radio Show

To find podcasts related to your expertise, submit a Google search on your topic. For example, I might Google, "inventor interviews" or "small business interviews" and approach them with a great idea for an interview.

When you participate in these interviews, not only is it a great experience, you are establishing a presence on the Internet. You are also adding to your search engine optimization (SEO) which, in turn, drives customers to your website.

MY FAVORITE TIP – Always be prepared for an interview. Ask the host if they would prefer sample questions you generate ahead of time or if they are going to send you their planned questions. Provide a bio. Send them your headshot for their website and promotion of the show. Make sure you know how long your interview will be and be ready to speak for that amount of time. Don't sell. The host won't forget why you are there, and you'll be able to talk about your business. Remember, you are there to provide content to their audience. This platform is a great way to build your list by offering something of value in exchange for someone's name and email list (more on opt-ins later in TIP #116).

TIP #110 – WHAT'S YOUR STORY?

As with magazines and television, send a targeted segment idea to the radio program. It's not you, your product, or your book that the show is interested in, it's what you can offer to entertain their audience. Tailor the way you share your expertise so it will be compelling to them.

I have a product-based business, yet I'm always asked to do radio interviews. It's the story they love; I had a vision, followed my passion, and brought my idea to fruition. Stories of getting a business off the ground through perseverance, and overcoming all the obstacles along the way, are inspiring. Hosts and audiences love these types of stories.

TIP #111 – FOLLOW THE RULES

A radio interview is a television interview, minus the visuals. The rules of being interviewed on television holds true for radio as well. Be authentic. Know your topic. Speak in sound bites. Be a gracious guest and be sure to get invited back. By practicing what I preach, every radio interview I have ever done has resulted in an open invitation to return.

TIP #112 – IT'S FREE HERE TOO

We've already learned about the free query services such as HARO and Source Bottle, but there is also a website specific to radio queries, www.RadioGuestList.com. Submit your information and once a day you receive radio queries of shows needing guests. Send in your concise, timely responses, and you will be on your way to becoming a regular radio guest.

TIP #113 – HOW DO I FIND YOU?

The easiest way to find radio stations is to Google the phrase "radio talk show" and keywords related to your subject matter. Research the results for a good fit, then find the station's contact information using the methods I've outlined.

Larger, nationally syndicated shows have a staff of producers. The person you want to contact is the "booker." This is the producer who schedules the guest experts and authors.

Local radio and podcasts may have just one producer and a host. Or, the host might handle everything, so there is only one person to contact.

You can also search www.Radio-Locator.com and RadioStation World.com, which are both excellent resources for finding radio shows.

Christina on Bloomberg Radio

TIP #114 – FOR STARTERS

You don't have to be great to start, but you have to start to be great.
~ Zig Ziglar

It's always a good idea, especially in your first few interviews, to ask if you can provide questions ahead of time. This way you will be completely prepared for the interview. Personally, I prefer not having preset questions so my interview can flow naturally. Some hosts and guests, however, prefer to go the prepared question route to make sure they have all bases covered.

If your interview is live, in-studio, always arrive early.

For a phone-in interview, always use a landline and disable call-waiting. You don't want to be mid-sentence when another call beeps in and cuts you out. Consider a headset as well. I gesture with my hands quite a bit when speaking, even on radio. It helps me articulate my story when I can walk and talk using both hands.

If you work from home, doing a radio interview is risky in terms of possible distractions or noise. If you have a dog, put your pup out of earshot. Put a sign by your doorbell asking people not to ring or knock during interview time. If your kids are home, remind them you are on a live call and cannot be distracted. I often lock myself in the basement for interviews. Lastly, turn off anything in the house that could cause background noise such as your cell phone, a ceiling fan, the radio, and television.

MY FAVORITE TIP – Have some water nearby just in case your mouth gets dry. Nobody will see the water bottle or even know if you sneak a sip during the interview.

TIP #115 – TALK THE TALK

Bring the best of your authentic self to every opportunity.
~ Brian Jantsch

As I mentioned above, you might provide questions ahead of time. Be prepared with your responses, but don't use notes. You want to be authentic and conversational, not rehearsed. If you're asked a question that you don't know the answer to, say you don't know, instead of fumbling your way through uncharted waters. And never answer with just a "yes" or "no." Always add more to your response.

Be a compelling guest, but let the host lead the discussion. It is their show and the audience is tuned in to hear them interview you. You are there to teach, not sell. As with television, don't drop your company name or website over and over. There will be a time to do that. Not once has a host forgotten to let me talk about my company and give my website along with any other information I wanted to share. Hosts will always make time for this promotion.

Last but not least, keep an eye on the clock. Give yourself the last several minutes to wrap up and have time to share your business information. If it's an eight-minute interview, know you're wrapping up your content at six minutes. Most syndicated shows are either eight or fifteen-minute interviews, while Podcasts are usually 30 minutes, sometimes even a full hour.

TIP #116 – GIVE A GIFT

Make the most of your on-air appearance and have a "freebie" or an opt-in available that you can send listeners to. This is something of value about your topic for which they will exchange their name and email address. It could be a pdf, a checklist, a guide, or an infographic. Ideally, you want an easy to remember custom URL like www.FreeGiftfromChristina.com.

Content is King

In order to establish yourself as an expert in your space, you must have content to show for it. The easiest way to do this is to blog. Having good content on your website allows you to check out when the media and/or potential customers check you out. There are also tremendous opportunities to guest blog or to have someone blog about you on a high-ranking site. This is the best-case scenario because you get to piggyback on their top search engine optimization (SEO) ranking. When someone searches about your topic, and you were covered in a high-ranking blog, it will come up early in the Google search results. This is not necessarily the case with a television appearance or a quote in a magazine. Take advantage of the power of blogs and what it means for SEO and search results on the Internet.

Remember, bloggers need regular fresh content just like other media. They welcome the opportunity to blog about businesses, products, books, and interesting stories. Another option is to guest blog for them. A quick Google search using your industry keyword(s) and "blog" should help you find some great resources.

If you are a product-based business, be prepared to send review samples to bloggers. Many blogs are actually product review sites and are a great way to get exposure to a large audience. Check their Alexa ranking (www.Alexa.com) first to make sure they are getting enough traffic to warrant you sending in a sample. The lower the number, the higher ranking the site.

I was approached by a fashion blogger from Mercedes Benz Fashion Week in New York who was in a walker boot. I sent her product for her boot, and in return she sent me several photographs of herself with professional models and celebrities. We were able to create a great marketing campaign around Fashion Week.

As for your personal blog, the time is now. Content is king! The more written and ideally video content you are putting on the Internet, the more secure your place is as the preeminent expert in your field. If the media is looking for an expert, they will certainly Google the topic; if you come up near the top, are branded well, and show that you have provided great content, the chances of them reaching out to you as their expert are significantly increased.

TIP #117 – LET'S GET THIS PARTY STARTED

You miss 100% of the shots you don't take.
~ Wayne Gretzky

There is no excuse for not starting a blog. If technology is your issue, here are some resources to help with starting a blog: www.TypePad.com, www.Blogger.com and of course if you have a WordPress site, www.WordPress.com you can add your blog to that site.

You know your subject matter. You started a business based on it. If you need help getting creative, think about the questions potential customers ask. This is a great way to create content. If one person is asking a particular question, it's likely someone else will have a similar question.

You don't have to reinvent the wheel with your blog. Go with what you know and consider doing some short videos that are transcribed as blog content.

It's all about getting information out on the Internet and establishing yourself as *the* expert in your field.

TIP #118 – ONCE IS ENOUGH

Post a blog article only once. Duplicate content must be avoided. If Google realizes you have uploaded the same information on various sites, they may lower your search engine optimization (SEO) rank. Write a post, upload it on your site or contribute to another blog, and then move on to another topic. If you do end up using an existing post, make considerable changes to the text so it doesn't appear to be duplicated content.

MY FAVORITE TIP - Save your best work for guest blogging sites with higher rankings to get more views on your best content.

TIP #119 – GIVE THEM WHAT THEY WANT

Longer form blog posts are more beneficial to search engine optimization (SEO). According to research done by the popular blogging site, *Medium*, blog posts should be no less than 300 words but over 1000 to rank higher on the search engines. The ideal blog post should be 1,600 words which equates to a 7-minute read.

According to *Forbes Magazine*: blog posts that have over 1,500 words are over 68% more likely to be shared on Twitter and over 22% more likely to be liked on Facebook (compared to shorter posts). The downside, however, is that longer posts are more difficult to write, and often readers prefer shorter content that is easier to digest.

So what should you do?

If you want to create frequent content on a wide variety of topics that prompts readers to take an action, the 300-word blog posts are ideal. If you want to create a piece of content that can really boost your SEO and user engagement, spend the time to create quality, long-form content that is over 1,000 words. Ideally 1,600 words.

TIP #120 – BE A DIAMOND IN THE ROUGH

It is important to make sure your content is 100% original and that you understand copyright laws before blogging.

Here is the link to the U.S. Government's Copyright Law website, https://www.copyright.gov/title17/. If you have questions or concerns, contact an attorney.

A free resource available to test your blog post to make sure Google will see it as original content that is not plagiarized is www.CopyScape.com. Copyscape will find any matches to existing content and let you know if what you've written is too similar to what someone else has already posted.

TIP #121 – BE A GUEST

*Either write something worth reading
or do something worth writing.
~ Benjamin Franklin*

I was not a writer, but I had to learn. The Internet is full of content and people looking to fill their pages. I have been asked repeatedly to guest blog, write articles, and offer content for other sites. Though it's been difficult for me to turn myself into a writer, it has been invaluable for creating links back to my website. This helps with search engine optimization (SEO) and generating new leads for my business. It is also establishing me as an expert in my industry.

Use Google and research the top blogs in your industry. Before you approach someone about guest blogging for them, find out what they've already published on their site and determine where you can fill in any voids on existing topics.

Many of the highest-ranking sites on the internet have opportunities for you to be a guest writer.

MY FAVORITE TIP – Remember when guest writing, make sure you use your top ranking keywords so that when the article is published it will link back to your site and increase your search engine optimization (SEO).

TIP #122 – SOCIAL BUTTERFLY

Make sure you have social media share buttons posted with each article so readers can easily tweet, post, and share them on social media sites. A simple plug-in to your website like WP Social Sharing, will allow you to add this feature.

TIP #123 – PAY IT FORWARD

Consider becoming a contributor on a high-traffic blog. Your article will gain a great deal more exposure on a site with millions of viewers than your own blog site. A great place to start is, www.Business2Community.com/become-a-contributor. Anyone can apply to become a contributor with no prior blogging experience.

MY FAVORITE TIP – Do your research about the blog and determine how you could contribute and/or fill-in on any topics they have not yet covered.

💡 TIP #124 – THE ROAD LESS TRAVELED

If you are a really good writer, consider applying to become a guest columnist in a magazine. Though the spots are few, if writing is your strength, this is a great way to get your message out to the masses while establishing your credibility in your field.

CASE STUDY - Dr. Marcie is a children's behavioral therapist in New York City. What I found was that Dr. Marcie is an amazing writer, but she wasn't writing with SEO in mind or writing for Google rankings. As a result, nobody was seeing her work. We found the right contacts at the parenting magazines in New York and sent them copies of her work. Within two weeks, she had a regular column in *New York Parenting Magazine*.

If you remember, the Presidential election between Hilary Clinton and Donald Trump was quite contentious. During the election, Dr. Marcie positioned herself as THE expert discussing, "How do you talk to your kids about what's going on in the election." She was seen as an expert through her writing which ultimately landed her on national television.

TIP #125 – STATS 101

Check out these blogging statistics:

- 53% of marketers say blogging is their top content marketing priority. (HubSpot).
- 43% of people admit to skimming blog posts.
- Websites with a blog tend to have 434% more indexed pages.
- Blog articles with images get 94% more views.
- The average word count of top-ranking content (in Google) is between 1,140-1,285 words.
- Marketers who prioritize blogging are 13x more likely to achieve a positive ROI on their efforts.
- Companies who blog receive 97% more links to their website.
- Blogs have been rated as the 5th most trusted source for accurate online information.

Telling stats aren't they? Blogging is vital to a company's promotion, whether it is on your own blog, someone blogging about you, or guest blogging on another site.

If you haven't entered the blogosphere, it's time.

You're Invited to a Cocktail Party

Social Media is about the people! Not about your business. Provide for the people and the people will provide for you. ~ Matt Goulart

When I first wrote about this topic in my first book back in 2014, I was very green when it came to social media. I still believed it might not catch on. Now, it is a *must* for any business! I currently have upwards of 75,000 followers. I am verified on Twitter. I actually get clients through social media. The really good news is that you really only have to be on one platform. Make sure you do that one platform really well and create valuable content that encourages engagement. If you are on every platform only posting occasionally and not engaging with your audience, you are going to lose your followers. Mari Smith, a.k.a. The Queen of Facebook, said it best, "If content is king then engagement is queen."

Remember the "social" in social media. This is how you engage with your followers. Think of it as a cocktail party. You aren't going to meet someone and propose marriage. So, don't hop on social media and start selling before you get to know your audience.

You also want to speak the language of the platform. Think of each social media platform as a unique country with a unique culture and their own language. Facebook can be longer posts, as people spend time perusing their Facebook page. Hashtags haven't really taken off on Facebook so when you use them there, it doesn't make sense to someone who only uses that platform. Use hashtags on Twitter and Instagram because that's how people will find you.

My number one tip is to not use a service that cross-posts the same piece of content on multiple platforms without modifying for each one. Remember, this isn't about posting content, it's about building relationships with your followers and creating engagement.

TIP #126 – WHAT IS IT ANYWAY?

> *Social marketing eliminates the middlemen,*
> *providing brands the unique opportunity to have*
> *a direct relationship with their customers.*
> ~ Bryan Weiner

Why should you have a presence on social media? What can it really do for your business? A ton! It builds your brand recognition (my top tip for PR). If you are posting good, quality content, it establishes you as an expert in your field. By generating this content, you are likely to attract more people to your site, who could potentially be new customers. You are reinforcing your subject knowledge with your existing followers. Becoming well-known on a particular topic via social media (i.e. being Google-able) also allows you to leverage yourself for media opportunities.

Another important factor of social media is its viral nature. In the blink of an eye you can become a household name. Look at the young boy, Ryan, who hosts Ryan Toys Review. At the age of seven he was making $22 million annually, has over 30 billion views and 20+ million subscribers on YouTube.

It is important to determine what your message or expertise is, and to be very clear about that message. Every single thing you post on social media has to go with that message. You should always be in alignment with your branding and your message. People lose respect and trust for you if you deviate from your message. Consistency breeds trust and reliability.

TIP #127 – ZUCKERBERG'S BABY

Thank you, Mark Zuckerberg, for Facebook. I love this platform both personally and professionally. With your personal Facebook Page you are able to connect and interact with friends and family, and the Facebook Company Page or Group allows you to chat with potential customers, actual customers and fans.

Your website is basically the face of your company, while your Facebook Business Page or Group is a way to interact with your followers.

In terms of getting publicity through Facebook, make sure you are sharing great content on your Business Page, particularly video. The media will search topics and it is not uncommon for the media to find their experts through Facebook.

Many people use their personal page for business. I strongly discourage this, and it is also against Facebook's terms of service. I have worked with several people who have had their personal Facebook pages shut down for this reason. To date, we have been unable to find a contact number or person to help restore the pages once they've been removed. Additionally, your friends and family likely don't want to see everything you are posting about your business so keep the business-related posts on the Facebook business page.

To create your company Facebook Business Page, go here, www.Facebook.com/pages/create.php. Remember to make sure your Facebook cover page is aligned and consistent with your overall branding.

MY FAVORITE TIP – Share content that is applicable to your friends and family from your business page to your personal page to subliminally remind them of what you do. It will come onto your personal feed with your business page name thus reminding people about your business.

EXPERT TIP - Facebook is extremely noisy in today's world, making it very challenging to stand out and reach your audience. Clarity is the name of the game here. Fill in the blank:

I am the trusted go-to source for _____. Then, create thumb-stopping content based on your expertise. Place a heavy focus on video and visual content. The good news is you don't always have to create brand new content of your own. You can become a master curator. That is, do the legwork for your audience and cherry pick the best articles, tips, and resources around your niche to help them. Express your own thoughts around the content you share; don't just share without adding your own spin. Your audience will connect deeper with you when they know you've done the research. They'll come to trust you implicitly when they know you have their back. They'll put you on 'See First' on Facebook, which is fantastic. This is free marketing right there. If you visit my own Facebook Page, you'll see this is my own exact approach. ~ Mari Smith, CEO Mari Smith International, Inc., Premier Facebook Marketing Expert, aka the 'Queen of Facebook,' Author, *The New Relationship Marketing* and Coauthor *Facebook Marketing: An Hour A Day*. Visit marismith.com/videokit.

TIP #128 – GOING LIVE

As of the date of publication of this book, there is no better way to gain views and following on a social media platform than by using live video. For some this is unnerving but as with anything, practice makes perfect and hosting videos will become muscle memory. Start picking up your phone, turning on the camera, and going live with valuable information about your industry. Become a trusted source in your space and gain more followers by using the live video feature.

TIP #129 – BLUEBIRD CAFÉ

If you are working with millennials or younger, you really must be on Twitter because that is where they are. Also, if you have a national product, service or brand, I recommend this platform as well. Most journalists can be found on Twitter and it is a great way to build relationships with them. Like, comment, and re-tweet their work on Twitter.

A helpful feature on Twitter is the ability to create lists. These can be used to keep track of journalists and find out what's important to them and what they are talking about. Not sure how to set that up? Go to https://help.twitter.com/en/using-twitter/twitter-lists for step-by-step instructions. Go to your press list daily and see what your target journalists are talking about and stay connected.

There is a great tool available to help find influencers on Twitter called Muck Rack at www.muckrack.com. This free site allows you to search for journalists by their publication or their subject matter. There are thousands of journalists who can be found on Muck Rack. Entering the "newsroom" allows you to see what is trending on Twitter at that moment and which journalists are tweeting about it. They also send out the Muck Rack Daily in an email, which analyzes what journalists are saying and keeps you informed on current hot topics and trends.

CASE STUDY – I happened to be up late one night watching my local FOX news. I saw a great story on a segment called, *The Next Great Thing*, that featured products. I tweeted at the anchor telling her I loved the story. She replied and said, "If you know of any product that might work on our segment, let me know." That is how I landed a segment on FOX for CastMedic. Watch it here, www.PRforAnyone.com/FOX5.

TIP #130 – PIN-IT

Pinterest is such a fun form of social media. You find products, ideas, and themes you love and save them on boards and share with people. It's like your very own *Oprah's List* of your favorite things. Pinterest is all about pictures, so it's the perfect forum to visually share what moves you.

People discount Pinterest for business but Pinterest is a search engine like Google, so it's different than other social media platforms. By using the right keywords, you have the ability to attract an enormous amount of traffic to a post and gain followers and potential customers through Pinterest. This platform doesn't require the type of engagement like the others do.

Want to build PR on Pinterest? Create a board and pin articles from bloggers or journalists who cover your topics. You should also pin articles written about you because this publicity helps the journalist gain additional exposure as well. Journalists are able to determine who is driving traffic to their site, so this extra effort will help you in establishing a relationship with the journalist.

Another way to get to know journalists and their interests is to focus on what they pin on Pinterest. Comment, re-pin, and "like" their posts to start building relationships.

Take advantage of organic search engine optimization (SEO) by using keyword optimization on Pinterest as well. When pinning, change the description of things you post to include your keywords. Take advantage of your Pinterest presence to drive people to your website.

EXPERT TIP – Start with the end in mind. Know what you plan to sell and think about the kind of content and freebie that you can create that's related to what you have to sell. There's power in niching down, especially on Pinterest. Don't try to be all things to all people. ~ Rachel Ngom, https://www.rachelngom.com

TIP #131 – FREEZE-FRAME

Instagram is quickly growing in popularity and for many businesses, is their number one platform. There are over one billion people who login to Instagram every single day. Almost 3/4 of those users are between the ages of 18 and 34 so if that is your target customer, you might want to really consider Instagram. Most celebrities, television personalities, hosts, and many producers are on Instagram as well. It's a great place to follow them and see what they are interested in and are talking about.

Determine who influences you, people who inspire you, who the thought leaders are in your industry, the experts in your field, and particularly the journalists in whom you are interested and follow them.

Often users discover who to follow on Instagram by applicable hashtags. Go to a resource like www.hashtagify.me or www.exporttweet.com and find out what hashtags are popular in your industry. Keep a list and cut and paste applicable hashtags to each of your posts. Every post should have at least ten hashtags.

There is a new feature on your profile called highlights which lives on the main page of your profile and allows you to share snippets about you and your business. Take advantage of these so people can click on a highlight and get to know you and what you do. You can check mine out at www.Instagram.com/christina.daves. Feel free to give me a follow as well.

EXPERT TIP – We have two tips from Instagram Expert, Zach Benson, of Assistagram who works with some of the top digital marketers in the world.

Tip #1 – Here's a tip for Instagram that very few people know about. Instead of putting your actual name in the "Name" field of your profile, choose three different keywords that best represent your niche. So if you're an author, it could be something like "Author Business Nonfiction". Because Instagram scans through the "Name" field when it displays search results, your account will gradually rank higher for those keywords and you'll get more engagement and followers.

Tip #2 – Here's my best tip about how to make your content trend. Instead of using hashtags that have millions and millions of posts like "#motivation", look for similar hashtags that have between 50K to 300K posts, like "#motivation💪". Do this by typing the hashtag into the "Search" field and then scrolling down until you find what you're looking for. By choosing a hashtag with fewer posts, your content will trend higher and you'll get more engagement.

TIP #132 – TELL ME A STORY

Another way to engage with your followers and let them get to know more about you is by using Stories. This is available on both Facebook and Instagram. These are short snippets of videos or images that you can put together in a slideshow that is live for 24 hours only and then they disappear. On Instagram, you can move your stories to your categorized highlights where they will stay until you delete them.

TIP #133 – ARE YOU LINKED IN?

LinkedIn is often overlooked as a powerful business tool. Personally, I think it is the most important platform we have to grow our businesses. It is geared strictly towards business and professional networking with over 575 million users. Imagine the network you can create.

The most important aspect of LinkedIn is to create a profile that stands out. You only have a few seconds to make a first impression. Use your best headshot. Remember that this is not Facebook so you don't want an image that shows you at Happy Hour or has your children in the picture. Make your headline stand out with what you do for others not just your title. Tell other LinkedIn users how you can benefit them. Most people aren't searching "CEO" or "President" unless they are headhunters so give them keywords that allows you to be found.

Your LinkedIn profile is basically your sales page, so make sure you are impressing anyone who stops by to check you out. This is about what you can do for them. Feel free to view mine as an example and connect with me at www.linkedin.com/in/Christina Daves.

Because LinkedIn is a professional site, it's a smart way to connect with people in the media. Remember what I've been saying throughout this book, journalists need you as much as you need them. If you are a good, credible source, why wouldn't they connect with you? I always connect via LinkedIn with anyone in the media who has either reached out to me or with whom I have connected elsewhere.

I have an impressive lineup of connections including producers, editors, freelance writers, radio hosts, and bloggers.

Once connected with someone from the media, I send a message or email thanking them for the connection. Depending on the outlet, I might share my expertise and explain how we could work together in the future.

MY FAVORITE TIP – Connect with every businessperson you come in contact with. You never know with whom they might be connected that could help you in the future.

EXPERT TIP - LinkedIn Tips for "Moving Out of Default" in Settings & Privacy

1. Under SETTINGS & PRIVACY, take some time to review.

2. Under ACCOUNT, ensure you have more than one Email Address attached to your LinkedIn Profile (have a personal email so you always have access/control to the email)

3. Under PRIVACY, first item is "Edit your Public Profile". If you click on Change you will see that you are able to EDIT Your Custom URL. (Highly encourage you to have your NAME and not the # 's that LinkedIn has assigned to you.)

YOU'RE INVITED TO A COCKTAIL PARTY • 147

4. Continuing under PRIVACY #3 "Who can see your Connections." If you click on CHANGE, it will open up and explain who can see other connections.

5. Finally, under PRIVACY, you will see #4 -"*Viewers of this Profile also Viewed.*" These are professionals who might have your same skill set or experiences. Do you want to have them listed on your LinkedIn Profile? Only you can answer that. If you visit mine, you will see that feature is NOT Listed. https://www.linkedin.com/in/debbiesaviano ~ Debbie Saviano, Founder, Women's Leadership LIVE

TIP #134 – GOING TUBING

You Tube is currently the 2nd most popular social media platform with 500 videos being uploaded every minute and over one billion hours of video watched every day.

Making videos is as easy as using an iPhone or comparable smartphone device. They all have really good video capability. Videos are a powerful way to connect with your audience, so it's important to start creating videos, posting and sharing them yourself. Ninety percent of all content consumed online now is through video so if you aren't using video, you are missing the boat.

Not sure what to post? Talk about your expertise. Share media exposure you've received. Do a video describing your product or service. And don't forget, YouTube has a live video feature now too so take advantage of the algorithms that come with using live video.

EXPERT TIP – Often as content consumers, we relate SEO to being connected to Google, right? There are plenty of search engines people use every day, from Yahoo to Bing. Many often forget that YouTube is the only *social media platform* that prioritizes SEO in its ability to find videos online. Its complexity is far stronger in reach than searching with Hashtags on Facebook or Instagram with billions of users and rising each year.

When you are first starting your YouTube channel, or just don't know what to do to be seen and rank on YouTube, there are 8 best practices to follow and take action with to become stronger than your competitors. In a previous study by *Search Engine Watch*, it was stated that people consume *"over 4 billion hours a month on YouTube alone!"* As generations become more drawn to their mobile devices to watch videos, life has become simplified with YouTube TV, Netflix, Hulu and more for on the go every-day use. So, why not put your content on the 2nd most searched online platform in the world for consumers to find you, and have the ability to impact more people?

8 Best Practices to Optimize Your YouTube Channel

1) It is Important to rename your video file using a target keyword.

2) Insert your keyword naturally in the video title.

3) Be sure to optimize your video description.

4) Tag your video with popular keywords that relate to your topic.

5) You must categorize your video.

6) Upload a custom creative branded thumbnail image for your video's result link

7) Use an SRT file to add subtitles & closed captions.

8) You must add cards and end screens to increase your YouTube channel's viewership.

~ Tamara Thompson, Broadcast Your Authority, www.BroadcastYourAuthority.com.

Christina with YouTube Founder, Chad Hurley

TIP #135 – AUTOMATION NATION

Social media is a noisy place and people are constantly on the platforms looking and scrolling. How do you actually get someone to see what you're posting? You have to post, a lot! In order to do that, you'll need to consider automation. It would be almost impossible for a person to post on Twitter over thirty times per day in hopes of someone seeing that one, particular tweet. Every platform has the ability to automate. Here are some of our favorites:

- Hootsuite
- Buffer
- Meet Edgar
- Later
- Social Oomph
- Cinchshare

There are many others to choose from. Look into them and see which ones you are comfortable with and start automating all of your evergreen content like blogs, guest blogs, media appearances, videos, and tips. Any and all of your existing content should be automated, and new content should be added regularly.

TIP #136 – 80/20 RULE

A standard rule of thumb for social media is to post good content or information 80 percent of the time, and then it's acceptable to self-promote the other 20 percent of the time.

Extra! Extra!

Here are a few extra tips that will help you in your quest for media. The process is simple, IF you do it consistently. Follow the formula and massively grow your business through media. I can't wait to hear your success stories!

TIP #137 – I THINK I CAN! I THINK I CAN!

> *Patience, persistence and perspiration make an unbeatable combination for success.*
> *~ Napoleon Hill, Author*

Please don't give up if you don't hear back on your first try. PR is a lesson in patience and perseverance. Prepare yourself for "no," but don't let it deter you. Keep trying different contacts and angles—always stay professional and on-topic—eventually, you will hear that "yes," and the rewards will be outstanding. I hear about 100 "no's" for every "yes." But when I get a "yes," it is usually a big one!

Just because you haven't gotten a response from someone to whom you are submitting, don't give up. Remember, they are receiving hundreds of submissions every single day. If you are submitting relevant, timely information, continue to do so. You never know when that reporter or producer is going to need your information or will want to do a story on your topic. Your goal is to be the one they think of when they are looking for timely, quality information on a particular topic. It's all about building relationships.

When I launched CastMedic, I was so excited and so passionate and thought the sky was the limit. It was a big hill to climb and I hit a lot of roadblocks along the way and it started to break me. I was actually a finalist for *Shark Tank* Season 2. I made it through all the initial applications and interviews. I talked to the producers regularly and I was sure I was going to Los Angeles. Then the call came that changed everything. Even though everyone I had worked with so far loved me and my energy, there had been a similar product for regular boots in Season 1 and the executives at Sony thought it was too similar. Just like that, my dreams were squashed.

That was the start of a very rough run for five months when nothing went my way. It was a Wednesday night in October, and I remember sitting in front of my laptop crying asking the Universe what else I could possibly do to get this business off the ground. We had mortgaged our house and I only had a few months of money left to make payments on all the maxed-out credit cards. I was getting really close to rock bottom.

I woke up the next morning to an email in my inbox from the *Steve Harvey Show*. It was from an old HARO query I had sent in in August about "Do you have a product you want to take to the next level – national television." They were just getting around to the segment. The first thing they needed was a video. It was early in the morning. I had young kids then and they needed to get off to school. The show needed my video in an hour. I did some quick thinking and was able to take my *Shark Tank* audition video and make some quick edits to make it work for them. After a day of phone interviews, they invited me to come on the show.

When I got there, I found out it was Steve's Inventor Competition, and only then did I find out about the $20,000 prize. Everything aligned that day and those awful five months led to a life-changing event – winning this contest. The show put CastMedic

Designs on the map. I sold a ton of product and the $20,000 gave my business the shot in the arm it needed to get to the next level. The biggest lesson I can share is, never ever give up!

MY FAVORITE TIP – Consistent, regular pitching is vital for PR success. It's rare to land your first media appearance with your first pitch. That being said, many of my clients have been covered right away so you never know what's possible.

CASE STUDY – My client, Dustin Fox, a new real estate agent, pitched his very first story to the *Washington Post Real Estate Section*. His article appeared within two weeks of sending his story idea into the paper. Within six weeks of the article being published, Dustin landed five listings in excess of one million dollars each. His first year in business, he sold over $24 million in real estate. He continues to use this one article to win listings.

TIP #138 – WHAT'S THE WORST THAT CAN HAPPEN?

Your mountain is waiting, So… get on your way!"
~ Dr. Seuss

A mantra I have lived by my whole life and have also raised my children with is, "Just ask! What's the worst they can say?" Send that story idea. Write that email. Call that producer. What is the worst that can happen? They say, "No, thank you." So you didn't get on when you wanted. The first "no" is the worst. I promise, they do get easier. And remember, that "no" is actually the start of a relationship.

I can't tell you how many incredible things have happened in my life just because I asked! When I first launched PR for Anyone® I really didn't have the credibility to teach people how to do this even though my system was working over and over and over again.

I asked top people in the media if I could interview them and get their opinions on what I was sharing with my audience.

I was able to interview an Oprah producer, the head producer of the Rachael Ray Show, the head of PR for Ronald Reagan's Administration, Peter Shankman (founder of HARO) and many, many more. These wonderful people volunteered their time to share their knowledge and authority, confirming my theories and made me credible in the space.

Interviewing Hoda Kotb of the *Today* Show was a complete game-changer for my business and that happened because I asked to do the interview. Both professionally and personally, my life is full of proof that great things can happen when you simply ask for them. What's the worst anyone can say?

TIP #139 – WHEN A "NO" ISN'T NO

There is no failure except in except in longer trying.
~ Elbert Hubbard

Handling your own PR takes a thick skin. You can't take "no" personally. Journalists receive hundreds of submissions every single day, sometimes thousands. If you hear back and it's a "no," thank them for their consideration and keep them as an active contact. When something else comes up or you have another idea, send it to them. Time and time again, people who work in the media have told me that as long as you are providing fresh content, they want to see it.

I'll share a few personal stories about hearing "no" and how they really were a "not now."

I met a radio host at an event, gave him an idea, and he said, "That's not really what we cover." I nicely asked if I could put together a formal idea for the show and send it in. He liked what I sent, booked me on the show, and I received the most amazing complement: the host was so engaged in our conversation that he missed a commercial break. He actually phoned me after the interview and said in twenty years of interviewing celebrities, authors, and prominent guests, he had never been so engrossed in an interview that he missed a scheduled break.

As I mentioned earlier, I was featured in *Vail Beaver Creek Magazine*. What I didn't tell you then is that I had submitted that idea a year prior to it being included in the magazine. The journalist loved the product but couldn't fit it in anything they were doing at that time. Then, when Picabo Street was in a medical boot, the journalist could add my products to her story to make it more entertaining and valuable to her audience.

TIP #140 – DRIP, DRIP, DRIP

About half of what separates successful entrepreneurs from the non-successful ones is pure perseverance.
~ Steve Jobs

If you have something pertinent or newsworthy to share, follow-up with anyone in the media you have made contact with. You never know who might be interested. Repeatedly, people in the media whom I've interviewed have told me that it's okay to continue to submit ideas. Just don't continue to submit the same idea to the same journalist. Odds are if they didn't respond, they're not interested in that particular idea or perhaps just not at that moment. However, submitting a new idea is fine and is welcomed.

CASE STUDY – It took five months of regular, consistent pitching to secure a segment on *Good Morning Washington*. I continued to send in new ideas every month from Valentine's Day to St. Patrick's Day to Spring Break to Mother's Day to Father's Day. Finally, a Summer Entertaining segment was approved in August and I have been doing regular television segments ever since that original air date, www.PRforAnyone.com/GMWAugust.

Christina's first appearance on Good Morning Washington

TIP #141 – IT'S ALL ABOUT THEM

Talk to someone about themselves and they'll listen for hours.
~ Dale Carnegie

Remember that you are trying to build relationships with the media. Avoid sending emails that appear to be spam. Always address an email personally with, "Dear John" or "Dear Mr. Smith." Let them know that you read their magazine or watch their show and how you see a fit. Talk about *them* before you talk about you. Let them know how you can help them. Odds are you probably won't get booked or have a story written your first time out of the gate. There's a good chance you won't even get a response, but if you do, you've started your relationship with that person.

TIP #142 – WHAT'S YOUR PLAN?

Make an annual PR plan broken down by month that includes who you are going to submit ideas to and when. Here are some suggestions of what to include:

- ❖ Every day—Review and respond to the free media query services and check their Twitter sites.

- ❖ 1st and 15th - check all the daytime talk shows for pertinent topics and guest suggestions. Where do you fit? Send in an idea.

- ❖ Go through the editorial calendars of the magazines you feel are a good fit and make note of when you need to send your idea. Put dates on your calendar so you don't miss an opportunity.

- ❖ If you are located in or near New York City, Los Angeles, or Chicago and are interested in television opportunities, include Craig's List in this plan.

- ❖ Look through the "non-traditional" calendar and determine what holidays you can align with your business and come up with unique story ideas and mark your calendar.

TIP #143 – NICE TO MEET YOU

Build relationships with anyone you work with in the media. When someone does respond to your idea, whether it's a "yes" or "no," you now have a relationship to foster with that media contact. Media people move around all the time. Once you have a relationship with a writer or producer, stay in touch. They might move to another publication or program that fits with your business or product, and they can use you in the future.

I was a guest on Federal News Radio, www.PRforAnyone.com/FederalNews, because the show producer had previously worked as a producer on the ABC station in Washington, D.C. when I was a guest. She moved to radio and wanted to share my story with that audience.

MY FAVORITE TIP – Early on with CastMedic Designs, I was interviewed for a blog on Examiner.com. At that point I was doing anything I could to gain exposure and at that time, they were one of the highest-ranking blogs. Two years later, the journalist who interviewed me had moved to *Forbes*. She emailed me and said, "I always loved your story. I'm at *Forbes* now and pitched it to my Editor. We'd love to write an article about you." www.PRforAnyone.com/ForbesArticle. Forbes gets 27 million unique views per month. This was a tremendous opportunity!

TIP #144 – ONCE IS NOT ENOUGH

Don't think that if you've been featured in a publication once that you are a "one and done." Different people write about different angles and by pitching various topics, you can find yourself repeatedly covered in the same media outlet.

I was featured in *Forbes* about CastMedic Designs in the article above. I was also featured in *Forbes* for PR for Anyone® in this article, www.PRforAnyone.com/ForbesPR.

Providing various valuable newsworthy topics allows you to be covered again and again in the same media outlet.

TIP #145 – CONNECT, CONNECT, CONNECT

If you want to win at networking, don't keep score.
~ Harvey Mackay

I am a firm believer in networking and connecting. The key to this is providing value to the people you meet. Usually when I attend networking events, it's all about what they can sell me instead of meeting me and listening to where we might be able to help one another. Create connection, provide value, and stay in touch. PR is all about who you know, and more often it's who they know.

TIP #146 – THANK YOU VERY MUCH

The smallest act of kindness is worth
more than the grandest intention.
~ Oscar Wilde

Always send a handwritten thank you note after you appear on any show or in a publication. Do not use email. Go the extra step and handwrite a note. I always send a note on a card with my company logo or on a piece of personalized stationery.

MY FAVORITE TIP – An inexpensive resource for custom stationery is Vistaprint, www.VistaPrint.com. They regularly have specials, so I joined their mailing list and wait for a great deal and then stock up.

TIP #147 – BEHIND THE CURTAIN

There are often both free and paid opportunities to attend a "meet the media" event and actually interact with journalists.

I attended an event hosted by the *Washington Business Journal*. At this event, I met not only many of the reporters, but also the editor. He was so happy to learn what I do and that I am educating businesses on how to effectively pitch the media. You can only imagine what he has seen during his career.

This introduction has led to many other conversations. I was able to open the door for a local law firm I was working with to land coverage in the *Journal*. Additionally, I was able to interview the editor for a column I write in a magazine. How much credibility did I gain when I was able to interview the editor of a top local newspaper on how to pitch him effectively?

Thanks for Your Time...

If you've made it here, you've made it! You're ready to start your quest for free publicity. I've so enjoyed watching the people I've shared with you in this book land publicity. Many ended up in the media in less than 30 days – some in less than seven days. I have watched landing media coverage completely transform a business.

Do some homework and figure out where your ideal customer is in terms of what they are listening to, reading, and watching. Then, go one-step further and see what types of stories those media outlets cover. Send in a pitch that fits their format and their demographic. Make sure you've got a good hook so they read your pitch. Find the right journalist to send it to. That's the Get PR Famous Formula and it works!

I wish you luck in your endeavors and hope you found my information, and what my amazing friends, mentors, and industry experts shared with you, helpful. There is no doubt in my mind that if you implement these practices, you will have success. People I have worked with have appeared on local and national television such as, *Dr. Oz, CNN, Good Morning America, The Today Show,* and *The View*. They have appeared in print in *Wall Street Journal, Washington Post, U.S. News and World Report, Shape, First for Women, Entrepreneur, Success, Forbes*, and many more.

Don't forget, I'm still on this journey with you. I am constantly promoting CastMedic Designs and PR for Anyone®. Since writing my first book, I have appeared in over 1,000 media outlets including outlets like the *Today Show,* affiliates of *ABC, NBC, CBS,* and *FOX, Forbes, Entrepreneur, Bloomberg Radio,* and so many more. Landing a regular segment on *Good Morning Washington* has been a dream come true!

Stay passionate. Be pleasantly persistent. Provide value and start building relationships with people in the media.

If I can do it, you can too!

Connect with me and please stay in touch. I'd love to hear if anything you implemented as a result of this book brought you great results.

Twitter – www.Twitter.com/prforanyone

Facebook – www.Facebook.com/prforanyone

LinkedIn – www.Linkedin.com/in/ChristinaDaves

Instagram – www.Instagram.com/Christina.Daves

Pinterest – www.Pinterest.com/prforanyone

> *It is never too late to be what you might have been.*
> *~ George Eliot*

About The Author

Christina Daves is a native Washingtonian. She attended Virginia Tech where she received a Bachelor of Arts with a double-major in Political Science and German. She resides in the suburbs of Virginia outside of Washington, D.C. with her husband. She has two adult children.

Christina's career as a serial entrepreneur debuted with an event planning company she started with two close friends. Their signature events, multi-stage outdoor concerts held in D.C., drew up to 10,000 attendees. The company's big claim-to-fame was booking the then unknown Dave Matthews Band for a concert at a beach bar in Delaware.

A few years later, Christina met her husband and decided that partying for a living was not conducive to married life or starting a family. So off she went to work for the father of one of her partners, still in the planning business, but a toned-down version that involved learning about utilizing land for real estate development rather than rock 'n roll.

Shortly after Christina learned the ropes, her mentor retired, and she was able to use her newfound knowledge to start a niche business performing feasibility studies for data centers. Fortunately, she lived in the area where AOL was headquartered. Their datacenter explosion kept her busy for many years.

During that time, Christina and her husband moved to the outer suburbs to a new housing development, where you often find a large number of houses but no established businesses. It was in 2002 that the datacenter industry really started slowing down. Always the entrepreneur and observing the need for retail in her area, Christina and her best friend decided to try their hands at a brick and mortar retail store.

With no experience in retail, other than knowing what kinds of things she and her friend liked to buy, they rented and renovated an historic house and stocked it with merchandise. The house was once a Civil War nursing station, believed to be haunted by a colonel who died there. The colonel must have approved of their retail store, *Details for the Home*, because he's never interfered and it remains a successful business today.

After having the time of her life running *Details for the Home*, Christina was torn over the time demands of a retail store and having two very active children. Difficult as it was, she opted to retire from the retail industry and sold her share of the store back to her best friend.

Christina spent 2009 to 2010 at home with her children, not working. She was pulling her hair out not having a business to run. Fortunately, in the summer of 2010, an unfortunate accident led to a brilliant business idea. Christina broke her foot and was placed in an ugly medical walking boot the day before heading to New York City, Fashion Capital of the World. Finding nothing available on the market to dress up the medically necessary boot, she launched CastMedic Designs, a company that designs and manufacturers fashion-forward accessories, allowing anyone suffering in a medical boot to introduce fun and fashion into their healing wardrobe.

She officially launched CastMedic Designs in early 2012. During that first year, she was named one of the *Leading Moms in Business* by Startup Nation. Christina was also chosen as *Steve's Top Inventor* during an inventor's competition on the nationally syndicated *Steve Harvey Show*. She was also named Entrepreneurial Rule Breaker of the Year sponsored by Microsoft.

Christina's success in independently publicizing CastMedic Designs resulted in her appearing in over 50 media outlets in her first year in business. She has even accessorized a few famous broken bones by outfitting celebrities with medical boot bling including Diana Ross, Carla Hall, and even an Olympic gold medal winning gymnast.

These amazing accomplishments led her to launch PR for Anyone®, a resource for small business owners, entrepreneurs, and authors. PR for Anyone® provides training, coaching and various programs and resources to help users easily and effectively generate their own publicity. Her passion is sharing her experiences with other small business owners and entrepreneurs to help them create their own PR success.

Christina now speaks to thousands of people a year, across the country, on how to generate buzz for their business. She has also trained thousands of people and as a result, together with her students, has generated over one billion views and over eight figures in sales from free publicity

You can reach her directly at Christina@PRforAnyone.com.

Websites:

www.ChristinaDaves.com

www.HealinStyle.com

www.PRforAnyone.com

www.ChristinaInspires.com

You're off to great places!
Today is your day!
Your mountain is waiting!
So… get on your way!
~ Dr.Seuss

Made in the USA
Middletown, DE
17 February 2020

84690566R00106